SMITHSONIAN MISCELLANEOUS COLLECTIONS.

165

MONOGRAPH

OF THE

BATS OF NORTH AMERICA.

BY

H. ALLEN, M.D.

ASSIST. SURGEON, U. S. A.

WASHINGTON:

SMITHSONIAN INSTITUTION:

JUNE, 1864.

ADVERTISEMENT.

THE following memoir, by Dr. Allen, is designed to exhibit the present state of our knowledge respecting the species of *Cheiroptera,* or bats, found in America, north of Mexico, and their general geographical distribution. It is based principally on the specimens in the Museum of the Smithsonian Institution, although the collections of the Philadelphia Academy of Natural Sciences and of the Museum of Comparative Zoology of Cambridge have also been consulted.

JOSEPH HENRY,
Secretary S. I.

SMITHSONIAN INSTITUTION,
WASHINGTON, April 26, 1864.

PHILADELPHIA:
COLLINS, PRINTER

TABLE OF CONTENTS.

INTRODUCTION.

Among the numerous agents which Nature employs for restricting the excessive increase of the insect world, the bats hold a conspicuous position. Eminently adapted to an animal regimen, the vast majority of these animals are exclusively insectivorous in their habits. Mosquitos, gnats, moths, and even the heavily mailed nocturnal *Coleoptera*, fall victims in large numbers to their voracious appetites. Certain members of the order, such as Flying Foxes (Pteropodidæ), are strictly frugivorous, it is true; and others, as the Dog-bat of Surinam (*Noctula leporina*), classified as an insect-eating bat, partakes occasionally of fruit in addition to its more animal diet; none of the species found in this country, however, are known to subsist on any other than insect food. In this respect they hold a decided relationship to certain birds, and it is interesting to observe how, under different circumstances, these widely separated animals serve us to the same end. The functions which the latter perform during the day, the former assume in the evening. The latter prey upon the diurnal insects, while the former feed exclusively upon the crepuscular and nocturnal kinds. The disappearance of the birds of day is a signal for the advent of the dusky host, which, as it were, temporarily relieve from duty their more brilliant rivals in guarding the interests of Nature.

But, while thus connected with birds in their position in the world's economy, bats have none of that grace of form, or beauty of coloring so characteristic of the others. Their bodies are clumsy and repulsive; their hues are dull and unattractive—nor can the eye dwell with pleasure upon their grotesque and awkward motions. This aversion—so universally evinced toward these little animals—is heightened by the associations of the time and place of their daily appearance. Attendant, as they are, upon the quiet hours of twilight, when the thickening gloom is conducive to the development of superstitious feeling, bats have always been associated with ideas of the horrible and the unknown. In olden times, when the imagination of the people exceeded the accuracy of their observations, it was one of the numerous monsters inhabiting their caverns and forests. It has done service in many a legend; its bite was fatal; it was the emblem of haunted houses; its wings bore up the dragon slain by St. George.

It is easy to trace from this early impression the permanent position that the bat, as an emblem of the repulsive, held in letters and the arts. It is mentioned in the Book of Leviticus as one of the unclean things. Its image is rudely carved upon the tombs of the ancient Egyptians. The Greeks consecrated it to Proserpine. It is part of the infernal potion of the witches in Macbeth, while Ariel employs it in his erratic flights. In art, its wings have entered largely into the creation of those composite horrors—evil spirits, nor have modern artists escaped from the absurdity of encumbering the Satan of Holy Writ with like appendages.[1] Of this association with the monstrous the intelligent observer ceases to take note when the finer beauties of structure develop themselves under his gaze. Upon acquaintance he learns, perhaps with surprise, that, in anatomical and physiological peculiarities, and zoological position, the bat is a subject for study worthy of the attention of the most contemplative. Indeed, no order of animals is more interesting, and none has received greater attention from the hands of savans.

The early pioneers of natural history were far astray in their endeavors to correctly define the nature and position of the bat.

"Some authors place bats among the birds, because they are able to fly through the air; while others assign them a position

---

[1] To this fancy of the ancients of placing the wings of a bat upon demons is happily opposed the sweet conceit of poets in adorning the figures of angels and cherubim with the wings of birds. The wing of a bat is sombre and angular—that of a bird is of delicate hues and replete with curves. It is therefore poetic justice to have the one become an emblem of the infernal as the other is an expression of the heavenly form.

among the quadrupeds, because they can walk on the earth. Some again, who admitted the mammalian nature of the creatures, scattered them at intervals through the scale of animated beings, heedless of any distinction excepting the single characteristic in which they took their stand, and by which they judged every animal. These are but a few of the diverse opinions which prevailed among the naturalists of former times, among which the most ingeniously quaint is that which places the bat and ostrich in the same order, because the bat has wings and the ostrich has not."[1]

Without reviewing the recorded errors of these observers, we will be content to call the attention of the reader to the following brief account of the structure of flying animals, so that the true position of the bat among them may be definitely fixed.

There are two distinct types of modification which the vertebrate skeleton has undergone in adapting the animal for flight, both of which depend upon some peculiarity in the structure of the anterior extremities; and in order to obtain a correct opinion of them we propose to cast a glance at each in turn.

Plan of bony structure of the wings of flying vertebrate animals.

a. Bones of carpus separated; flight maintained by dermal expanse	I. Wing membrane supported by all fingers— *Bats* (Vespertilio), order of Mam.
	II. Wing membrane supported by the 4th finger only (which is immensely developed), the others remaining free— *Pterodactyles*, order of Rept.
b. Bones of carpus united; flight maintained by dermal appendages	III. Bones of metacarpus 2–3 in number— Feathers not radiating— *Living birds* (Aves)—class.
	IV. Bones of metacarpus 4 in number— Feathers radiating— *Archæopteryx* (Aves)—subclass.

[1] Wood, Nat. Hist. I (Mam.), 114.

a. I. The Bat, in which the humerus is long and slender, with a small pectoral ridge. Ulna rudimentary, attached to the curved radius, which constitutes the bulk of the forearm; carpus composed of 6 bones; the metacarpal bones 5 in number, separate and distinct; the phalanges generally 2 in number; thumb, and in some the index finger surmounted by a claw.

II. The Pterodactyle, in which the humerus is short and straight, very broad at head, with angular and prominent pectoral ridge; ulna and radius distinct, of nearly equal size; carpus composed of 5 bones; metacarpus of 4 bones, separate and distinct; 1st finger with 3 joints, 2d with 4, 3d with 5, 4th with 4 joints, all provided with claws, with the exception of the 4th, which is remarkable for the extraordinary development of its several joints. It is from this last mentioned finger to the base of the foot that the skin was stretched by which the animal was enabled to fly.

b. III. The Bird, in which the humerus is curved, more or less slender; pectoral ridge prominent, not angular; ulna large, curved, not united with the slender and more diminutive radius; carpus of 2 bones; metacarpus of 2, sometimes of 3 bones—the first being small and cylindrical, the other two of larger dimensions and united so as to form a bone resembling the bones of the forearm; ulnar phalanx of 1 joint, united to the radial which is composed of 2.

The power of sustaining flight not dependent upon the expansion of skin, but upon the excessive development of dermal appendages (feathers).

IV. The Archæopteryx[1] agrees with the typical bird in general particulars, but differs in the number of the metacarpal bones, which are here 4 in number: the 1st and 2d are slender, free and separate from one another; the 3d and 4th bear considerable resemblance to those of extant birds, in being large, stout, and closely approximated; but are not, however, united.

Flight is supposed to have been maintained in the same manner as in living birds.

---

[1] *Archæopteryx lithographica*, H. von Meyer, a fossil of the Lower Jurassic formation of Germany, obtained from the lithographic stone at Solenhofen. It was first made known to science by Prof. Wagner, at a meeting of the Mathematico-Physical Class of the Royal Academy of Sciences of Munich, in 1861, and was more minutely described, by H. Hermann von Meyer, in Jahrbuch für Mineralogie, 1861, 561.

This remarkable fossil, which is at present exciting such profound attention among anatomists, combines the characters of the bird and the reptile so intimately that it was for a time a matter of doubt to which

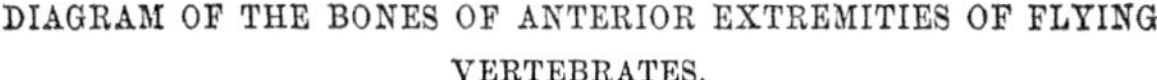
DIAGRAM OF THE BONES OF ANTERIOR EXTREMITIES OF FLYING VERTEBRATES.

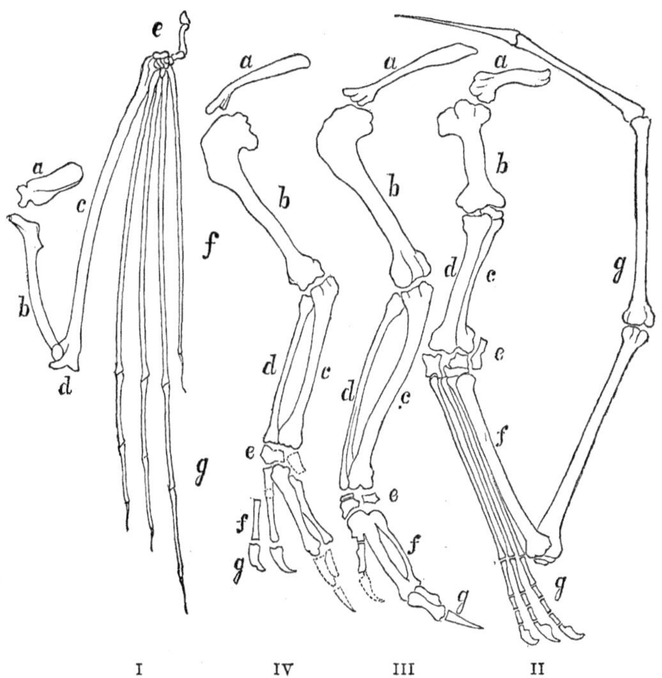

I. Bat.—*a.* Scapula. *b.* Humerus. *c.* Radius. *d.* Rudiment of ulna anchylosed to radius. *e.* Carpus. *f.* Metacarpus. *g.* Phalanges.

II. Pterodactyle.—References the same as in Fig. I.

III. Bird.—References as in Fig. I. The dotted outline of the second ungual phalanx indicates the occasional occurrence of a claw at this point. The majority of birds are without it.

IV. Archæopteryx.—References as in Fig. I. The dotted outlines seen at carpus and the terminal phalanges are restored portions.

In addition to the instances already given, certain fishes, as the *Exocœtus* and *Dactylopterus*, possess the power of sustaining true flight. The mechanism that lifts the body of the fish from the water, and upholds it for a short time in the air, is obtained in the pectoral fins, which, in these animals, are enormously developed. The structure of these fins is homologous to that of the anterior extremities of other vertebrates—their form alone being modified to adapt the animal to the medium in which it is placed. Thus we have, in each great subdivision of vertebrate animals, a representative capable of sustaining flight.

Another somewhat similar modification of the animal economy is met with in a few animals of arboreal habits. Here a peculiar arrangement of the skin is observed, which enables the possessor to break the force of downward leaps. In the Flying Lemur (*Galeopithecus*), in the Flying Squirrel (*Pteromys*), and in the Flying Opossum (*Petaurista*), the furred skin extends laterally from the sides of the body, and is attached to anterior and posterior extremities at the metacarpal and metatarsal regions respectively. The only instance of osteological development is obtained in the Dragon (*Draco volans*), a small lizard from Sumatra, in which long, transverse processes from either side of the lumbar vertebræ support a thin membranous growth which is capable of being opened and shut by means of muscles attached to the bony frame-work.

Anatomy.—From the consideration of the mechanism of the wings of bats, it is an easy transition to speak of their anatomy.

The bones of *Cheiroptera,* though incapable of receiving air from the surrounding medium, are nevertheless of very light

---

class it could be assigned. Its peculiarities consist of a continuation of the bones of the vertebral column posteriorly to the number of twenty segments, thus creating a tail seven inches in length; of the metacarpal bones, being composed of four bones instead of two or three as in living birds; and of the reptilian character of the pelvis.

For descriptions concerning this curious animal the reader is referred to the original paper by M. von Meyer, *loc. cit.;* an article in *The Intellectual Observer*, for Dec. 1862 (with plate), by Wm. H. Woodward; an article in *Amer. Journ. Sci. and Arts*, 2d series, XXXV, May, 1863, 129 (Prof. Dana); an article in *Phil. Trans.* CLIII, part I, 1863, 33, pl. 1 to 4 (Prof. Owen). The last mentioned paper is the most complete on the subject, and is accompanied with a handsome full size plate of the fossil.

It is from this memoir that the outline engraving on the opposite page has in part been taken.

structure. The skeleton of a bat is expressive of lightness and tenuity. The bones of the common Brown Bat (*V. subulatus*), from which this description is taken, weighed but eleven grains.

The *skull* is of proportionate large size, rounded at cranium. The parietal crest, generally faintly produced, is frequently entirely absent; at the superior angle of occipital bone a faintly defined triangular patch is seen in those skulls where the temporal fossæ on either side have not extended quite the length of the side of cranium. Orbit incomplete; temporal fossæ very large; zygomata perfect, generally slightly curvilinear, somewhat depressed in centre. Anterior nares large, sub-circular, extending back on the palate to a level with the canine teeth. Intermaxillary bones rudimentary and not meeting in front. The bones of the cranium are without diploe, and the interior of the skull without tentorium. Auditory bullæ (viz., the circular appendages to the external meatus) very large. Occipital condyles broad; foramen magnum large, sub-oval, somewhat depressed. The maxillary bones are stout, and support all the teeth, excepting the incisors, which are held in position by the inter-maxillary bones.

The *lower jaw* is stout, receding at symphysis, where it is very high, and extends backwards to a level with the 2d premolar tooth; coronoid process high, blunt, strongly marked externally to its base with the concave surface for the insertion of temporal muscle. The anterior border is vertical, the superior and posterior are slightly oblique, ending in the condyloid process; the articulating head of which is arranged transversely to the axis of the bone. The ramus of the jaw is turned slightly outward, and is thin and compressed. A large hamular process is conspicuous immediately inferior to the articulating surface.

The *teeth* are of variable number—being in some species as low as 30, in others as high as 38. This variation, combined with differences in their contour, furnish characters of great importance in the classification of these animals. The principal differences are seen in the number of the incisors and molars. The usual number of incisors is 4 in the upper, and 6 in the lower jaw. The number is never in excess of this, though frequently falling short of it. Thus, in some genera there are but 2 incisors above and 4 below; or there may be none above and but 2 below. When the number in the upper jaw is confined to 2 teeth the central incisors are wanting. The number in the lower jaw is always 6 in the family *Vespertilionidæ*, with the exception of the Californian genus *Antrozous*, which has here but 4 incisors. In this particular it shows evidence of its affinity with the family *Phyllostomidæ*, in which 4 incisors in the lower jaw is the normal number.

The molars are of two kinds: the true molars, and the false or premolars. The former are the larger and situated most posteriorly, the latter are small, placed between the true molars and the canines, and appear to unite the characters of both these teeth. The premolar adjoining the first molar bears a stronger resemblance to the grinders than to the premolar adjacent to the canine, which shows decided resemblance to the eye tooth. The number of molars (true and false) in any bat never exceeds 6 above and 6 below. In any diminution of this number the first premolar is always wanting.

The minute description of the teeth is reserved for the remarks under each species. It will be well in this place, however, to define the true molars, and since they are not subject to any material variation in shape no mention of them will be made in the text.

The true molars are 3 in number, both above and below. In the upper jaw they are of a sub-triangular shape, wider than long, their bases being outward, and their apices rounded and blunt. The first and second teeth have two V-shaped cusps upon the articulating surface of the crown—the anterior border of each cusp being more prominent than the posterior. The union of these two cusps constitutes what is known as the W-shaped crown. This irregularity is occasioned by the sinuate incurving of the enamel of the tooth; it eminently adapts the organ for the mastication of insect food. The inner portion of the articulating face is lower than the outer, is of a rounded shape, and is furnished with but one cusp, which, however, placed immediately behind the anterior triangular cusp, runs obscurely backwards to behind the posterior cusp, giving these teeth the appearance of being quadri-cuspid. The third molar, much smaller than the preceding, has a straight anterior and a rounded posterior surface; the external face of crown is irregular and sinuate, posterior unicuspid.

In the *lower jaw* the molars are of equal size. They are longer than wide. Each tooth is made up of two V-shaped cusps, their bases lying inwards, their apices very acute. The anterior cusp is wider and somewhat higher than the posterior.

The *vertebral column* is remarkable for the absence of any prominent processes. The cervical vertebræ are little more than slender rings of bones surrounding a spinal marrow of unusual width. The dorsal are also very uniform in appearance, each bone having its sides furnished with a slightly elevated tubercle. The *ribs* attached to them are relatively broad, very long, and much curved, thus giving the thorax a somewhat compressed appearance. The first rib is remarkable for its extreme breadth, especially at the point where it articulates with the sternum, being here twice the width of the clavicle. The *sternum* is of great strength. The manubrium is markedly crested, broad and flat at base whence two blunt, obtuse alæ spring from either side to articulate with the clavicle and first rib. The gladiolus and xyphus are large and robust; the latter has upon its inferior extremity an expanded cartilaginous piece, which is continuous with the linea alba. The object of this excessive development of the sternum is evident: the immense power employed in the maintenance of flight necessitating the presence of strong osseous points for attachment of the muscles. The *clavicle* is long, much arched, and slightly flattened from before backwards. The *scapula* is of a sub-rhomboid shape. At the upper third of its dorsal surface the dorsal spine runs obliquely forwards and terminates in the large acromion. The coracoid process is also conspicuous, and projects at right angles from the scapula parallel with a similar process from the internal superior angle of the shoulder blade. The *humerus* is long, cylindrical; head small, scarcely longer than shaft; two processes before and behind the articulation are observed for the insertion of the scapular muscles. The inferior extremity has but one articular facet. The forearm consists of the *radius* alone, the *ulna* being entirely absent or confined to a mere rudiment attached to the upper posterior part of the radius. The radius is slightly arched, much larger than humerus, and like it without any process. The *carpus* is composed of 6 bones, of which the largest supports the radius. The bones of the *metacarpus* are greatly developed in length, constituting the bony frame-work upon which the wing membranes are stretched. The thumb has two joints, the terminal one of which is surrounded by a claw, the others having generally three joints each—long and cylindrical. The *pelvis* is slender and narrow. The ilii are elongated, not widened, and markedly convex on outer surfaces; ischia relatively large, and converging; pubis rather slender. The ossa innominata are readily disunited at symphysis, their union to the sacrum being firmer. Obturator foramen large and elliptical. Both *femur* and *tibia* are long cylindrical bones, presenting no features of interest. The *fibula* is slender, acuminate and imperfect; it arises from the base of the tibia, and terminates midway up that bone. By the partial eversion of the lower extremity it appears to lie to the *inner* side of the tibia. The *toes* are five in number and armed with sharply curved claws; the calcaneum is enormously developed as a spicula of bone, running obliquely downwards and inwards towards the tail, and inclosed within the border of the interfemoral membrane. The termination of this bone is abrupt in some species, in others its extremity blends with the free edge of the membrane. The *tail* is composed of nine joints in the majority of bats, which diminish in width from above downwards; the tip of the tail may or may not be included in the interfemoral membrane.

Mr. Thomas Bell, in reviewing the osteology of the bat, uses the following language:—

"The whole of this structure is so perfectly adapted to the peculiar habits of the animals as to require no comment. The great development of the ribs, sternum, and scapula for the attachment of strong muscles of flight; the length and strength of the clavicle; the extension of all the bones of the anterior extremity, all admirably tend to fulfil their obvious end."—*Cyclopedia of Anat. and Phys.*, art. *Cheiroptera.*

The digestive apparatus is very simple, as might be supposed from the nature of the food upon which these animals subsist. The stomach is simple, with small fundus. The intestine is short, measuring but one and a half times the length of the body, and in many species without a cæcum.

The nervous system is highly developed, especially the special senses of hearing and of touch. The ears, both internally and externally, are highly perfected. The cochlea are disproportionately large as compared with the size of the semicircular canals. The ampullæ, as already seen, are very large. To this osseous structure, for the reception of sound, is added the complicated auricle with which all insectivorous bats are provided. These are frequently much larger than the head, and of great variety of shapes: their variations of form being of great importance in classification.

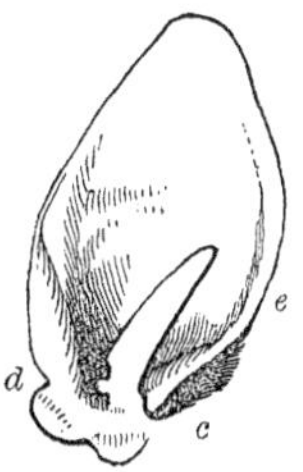

The internal border is generally much curved, and terminates in an obtuse or acute projection, called *the internal basal lobe* (*c*); the external border of the ear is of an irregular convex contour, and ends anteriorly in a blunt and thickened fold of membrane—*the external basal lobe* (*d*).[1] The tragus, or oreillon (*e*), is an upright growth of membrane extending from the base of the auricle up the centre of the external ear. The function of this appendage is not known; it probably acts as a valve to prevent foreign substances entering the ear, or to prevent the volume of sound received from such a large auricle in impinging too forcibly upon the delicate tympanum.

The nose is also frequently the seat of extensive dermal growths. These appendages, situated about the nostrils, may be simple upright, triangular folds of skin, or they may be exceedingly complicated in structure. No North American bat, with but one exception (*M. californicus*), has such a development. Though the external ear is evidently intended to augment the sense of hearing, there is some doubt whether the nose leaves hold the same relation to the olfactory sense. These growths are composed of reduplications of skin, and are not related to the lining membrane of the nose. They are probably the agents for augmenting the sense of touch alone, and in this way act conjointly with the wing membranes.

It is in this latter structure that the sense of touch chiefly resides. The bones of the extremities being covered on either side with an enduplication of skin, form a frame-work upon both sides

[1] In the above cut the external basal lobe has been turned backwards to disclose the base of tragus.

of which the papillæ of touch are extensively distributed. This function, in many places, is probably aided by the delicate hairs which are sparsely distributed linearly upon the under surfaces of the membranes. These may perform a function analogous to that observed in the labial whiskers which are so prominent in the *Felidæ*. Spallanzani was the first to notice the high development to which this sense had been brought in these animals. His experiment is well known, but will bear repetition here:—

"In 1793 Spallanzani put out the eyes of a bat, and observed that it appeared to fly with as much ease as before, and without striking against objects in its way, following the course of a ceiling, and avoiding, with accuracy, everything against which it was expected to strike. Not only were blinded bats capable of avoiding such objects as parts of a building, but they shunned, with equal address, the most delicate obstacles, even silken threads, stretched in such a manner as to leave just space enough for them to pass with their wings expanded. When these threads were placed closer together, the bats contracted their wings, in order to pass between them without touching. They also passed with the same security between branches of trees placed to intercept them, and suspended themselves by the wall, &c. with as much ease as if they could see distinctly."—*Godman's Amer. Nat. Hist.* I, 1831, 57.

Habits.—The habits of these animals are but little known. We possess a general knowledge that they are of nocturnal and crepuscular habits; that they feed upon night insects; that they frequent in their hours of repose secluded retreats in common with other nocturnal animals. To this circumstance, as much as any other, our ignorance of their habits is chiefly due. The darkness and unpleasant surroundings of their haunts are sufficient obstacles to cool the ardor of the most enthusiastic naturalist. Opportunities are offered occasionally, however, to observe their flight, and their habits in repose, by their accidental entrance into the open apartments of our dwellings in warm weather.[1]

[1] In this connection I take the liberty of quoting from Mr. Audubon's "Eccentric Naturalist," a sketch which appeared in the "Ornithological Biography" of that author. The hero of this sketch is well known to have been M. Rafinesque. The incident narrated was one of a series of adventures equally ludicrous which Mr. Audubon graphically narrates:—

"When it was waxed late I showed him to the apartment intended for

Under these circumstances they can be readily caught, and although bearing captivity poorly, can yet with care be sustained for some time. In this condition they will take small pieces of raw meat with avidity, though—strange as it may appear—refuse to partake of insects. They appear to drink largely of water. A small Brown Bat, which I once caught and caged, would lap up water eagerly when all food was refused.

The first act of the bat, after emerging in the evening from its retreat, is to fly to the water. The following account illustrating this peculiarity, as well as showing the enormous numbers in which these animals will live together, is of great interest. It is from the pen of M. Figaniere, Minister to this country from Portugal, in a letter addressed to Prof. Henry, Secretary of Smithsonian Institution :—

"In the winter of 1859, having purchased the property known as Seneca Point, on the margin of the Northeast River, near Charlestown, in Cecil County, Maryland, we took possession of it in May of the next year. The dwelling is a brick structure covered with slate in the form of an **L**, two-storied, with garret, cellars, and a stone laundry and milk house attached. Having been uninhabited for several years it exhibited the appearance, with the exception of one or two rooms, of desolation and neglect, with damp, black walls, all quite unexpected, as it had been but very slightly examined, and was represented in good habitable condition, merely requiring some few repairs and a little painting.

"The boxes, bundles and other packages of furniture which had preceded us, lay scattered around and within the dwelling: these, with the exception of some mattresses and bedding for

---

him during his stay, and endeavored to render him comfortable, leaving him writing material in abundance. I was indeed heartily glad to have a naturalist under my roof. We had all retired to rest. Every person I imagined was in deep slumber, save myself, when of a sudden I heard a great uproar in the naturalist's room. I got up, reached the place in a few moments, and opened the door, when, to my astonishment, I saw my guest running about the room naked, holding the handle of my favorite violin, the body of which he had battered to pieces against the walls in attempting to kill the bats, which had entered by the open window, probably attracted by the insects flying around his candle. I stood amazed, but he continued running round and round, until he was fairly exhausted; when he begged me to procure one of the animals for him, as he felt convinced they belonged to a 'new species.'"

immediate use, were hastily arranged for unpacking and placing in order at leisure. The weather, which was beautiful, balmy and warm, invited us towards evening to out-door enjoyment and rest after a fatiguing day of travel and active labor; but chairs, settees and benches were scarcely occupied by us on the piazza and lawn, when to our amazement, and the horror of the female portion of our party, small black bats made their appearance in immense numbers, flickering around the premises, rushing in and out of doors and through open windows—almost obscuring the early twilight, and causing a general stampede of the ladies, who fled covering their heads with their hands, fearing that the dreaded little vampires might make a lodgment in their hair.

"This remarkable exhibition much increased our disappointment in regard to the habitable condition of our acquisition, and was entirely unexpected, inasmuch as the unwelcome neighbors were in their dormant state and ensconced out of sight, when the property was examined previous to purchase. With their appearance and in such immense numbers the prospect of immediate indoors arrangement and comfort vanished; the paramount, the urgent necessity was to get rid of such a nuisance as quickly as possible; and the question was by what means could this be accomplished. Our scientific friends and acquaintances, both in New York and Philadelphia, were consulted, various volumes of natural history were examined in order to ascertain the peculiar habits of the vermin, but we derived no effectual consolation from these sources. One of our friends, indeed, sent us from New York an infallible exterminator in the form of a receipt obtained at no inconsiderable cost: strips of fat pork saturated with a subtle poison were to be hung up in places where the annoying 'creatures' did most congregate; of this they would surely eat, and thus 'shuffle off their mortal coil.' How many revolving bat seasons it might have required by this process to kill off the multitude, the urgency of the case would not allow us to calculate, and the experiment was therefore abandoned.

"Evening after evening did we patiently, though not complacently, watch this periodical exodus of dusky wings into light from their lurking places one after another, and in some instances in couples and even triples, according as the size of the holes or apertures, from which they emerged, in the slate roofing would permit. Their excursions invariably commenced with the cry of the '*whippoorwill*,' both at coming evening and at early dawn; and it was observed that they always first directed their flight towards the river, undoubtedly to damp their mouse-like snouts, but not their spirits, for it was likewise observed that they returned to play hide and seek, and indulge in all other imaginable gambols: when, after gratifying their love of sport and satisfying their voracious appetites (as the absence of mosquitos and gnats testified), they would re-enter their habitation, again to emerge at the first signal of their feathered trumpeter. I thus ascertained one very important fact, namely, that the bat, or the species which annoyed us, ate and drank twice in twenty-four hours. Such appeared their habit, such therefore was their indispensable need. Upon ascertaining this fact, after having tried suffocation by the fumes of brimstone with only partial success, I concluded to adopt a more efficient plan of warfare; and for this purpose commenced by causing all the holes, fissures in the wood-work, and apertures in the slating to be hermetically sealed with cement: this put a stop to their egress; but to avoid their dying by starvation and deprivation of water, which would manifold increase the annoyance by adding their dead to their living stench, I ordered apertures of about two feet square to be opened in the lathe and plastered partition on each side of the garret windows, and also in the ceiling of every garret room; lastly, when the bats' reveille was sounded by the bugle of the *whippoorwill*, all the hands of our establishment, men and boys, each armed with a wooden implement (shaped like a cricket bat), marched to the third floor, 'on murderous deeds with thoughts intent:' a lighted lantern was placed in the middle of one of the rooms, divested of all furniture, to allure the hidden foe from their strongholds. After closing the window to prevent all escape into the open air, the assailants distributed at regular distances to avoid clubbing each other, awaited the appearance of the bats enticed into the room by the artificial light and impelled by their own natural craving. The slaughter commenced, and progressed with sanguinary vigor for several hours, or until brought to a close by the weariness of dealing the blows that made the enemy bite the dust, and overpowered by the heat and closeness of the apartment. This plan succeeded perfectly. After a few evenings of similar exercise, in which the *batteurs* became quite expert in the use of their weapon, every wielding of the wooden bat bringing down an expiring namesake, the war terminated by the extermination of every individual of the enemy in the main building. However, there still was the cock-loft of the laundry, which gave evidence of a large population. In this case I had recourse to a plan which had been recommended, but was not carried out in regard to the dwelling-house. I employed a slater to remove a portion of the slating which required repairing. This process discovered some fifteen hundred or two thousand bats, of which the larger number were killed, and the remainder sought the barn, trees, and other places of concealment in the neighborhood.

"In the main building nine thousand six hundred and forty bats, from actual counting, were destroyed. This was ascertained in the following manner: After the battling of each evening the dead were swept into one corner of the room, and in the morning, before removing them to the manure heap, they were carefully counted and recorded; many had been killed before and some few after the reckoning was made, and were not included in it, nor were those killed under the adjoining laundry roof. The massacre commenced by killing fewer the first evenings, the number increasing, and then diminishing towards the end; but it was generally from fifty or a hundred, up to six hundred and fifty—the highest mortality of one evening's work—dwindling down to eight, five, three, and two.

"This species of bat is generally small, black, and very lively. Some smaller than the ordinary size were found, probably young ones, and one or two larger, supposed to be grandfathers, of a reddish hue, which was thought to be from age. These vermin were generally more or less covered with a small sized bug, not very dissimilar to the common chinch, but of a different species. As previously stated, the bat has a very disagreeable odor, which also pertains to its ejection.

"The manure, as well as the bodies of the slain, was used to fertilize the flower and vegetable garden, and thus, in some degree, they served to compensate us for the annoyance to which we had been subjected. The manure, however, required to be applied with caution, since, if used in too large a quantity, it appeared to burn the organism of the plants.

"To remove the very disagreeable odor which remained in the upper part of the house, various kinds of disinfectants were employed with some advantage; but the most effectual method resorted to was that of opening holes of about four inches square, two at each gable end, to permit a current of air to pass through. These holes were covered with iron gauze, to prevent the re-entrance of any of the remainder of the army of the enemy which might hover around the premises.

"At the end of five years the odor has now nearly disappeared, being hardly perceptible during a continuance of very damp weather."

The fact mentioned above of the numerous parasites infesting bats is perhaps the most revolting feature in these creatures. The enormous population of *Acari* found upon their bodies is due to the great generation of animal heat in their close haunts, a condition conducive to a rapid increase of all kinds of vermin. In this country the common bed-bug (*Cimex lectularis*) is frequently found upon their fur. The entrance of a bat, with its precious burden, into the open window of a farm house is the solution of that frequently propounded question of the despairing housewife: "Where *can* the bugs come from?"

Of individual anecdotes of bats we have but few examples. The following, illustrating the maternal instinct, is taken from Godman's Nat. Hist. I, 1831, 56. It is narrated by Mr. Titian Peale:—

"In June, 1823, the son of Mr. Gillespie, the keeper of the city square, caught a young Red Bat (*L. noveboracensis*), which he took home with him. Three hours afterwards, in the evening, as he was conveying it to the Museum, in his hand, while passing near the place where it was caught, the mother made her appearance and followed the boy for two squares, flying around him and finally alighted on his breast, such was her anxiety to save her offspring. Both were brought to the Museum—the young one firmly adhering to its mother's teat. This faithful creature lived two days in the Museum, and then died of injuries received from her captor. The young one, being but half grown, was still too young to take care of itself, and died shortly after.'

ARTIFICIAL KEY TO THE GENERA.

I. Istiophora.

(Bats with upright appendage on nose.)

Megadermatidæ.

Nose leaf simple, triangular, acuminate. . . *Macrotus.*

II. Gymnorhina.

(Bats without upright appendage on nose.)

A. Nostrils circular; wing membranes narrow; tail either much longer or much shorter than interfemoral membrane . . . Noctilionidæ.

Lips grooved . . . . . . *Nyctinomus.*

B. Nostrils subelliptical; wing membranes ample; tail inclosed in interfemoral membrane—the final joint in some instances exserted . . . . Vespertilionidæ.

a. Two incisors in upper jaw.

† Six incisors in lower jaw.

* Interfemoral membrane more or less hairy . . . *Lasiurus.*

** Interfemoral membrane not hairy . . . . *Nycticejus.*

‡ Four incisors in lower jaw . . *Antrozous.*

b. Four incisors in upper jaw.

† Molars $\frac{6}{6}$; internal basal lobe of ear acute . . . . *Vespertilio.*

‡ Molars less than $\frac{6}{6}$; internal basal lobe of ear rounded.

* Nose with two symmetrical excrescences . . . *Synotus.*

** Nose without excrescences . *Scotophilus.*

MONOGRAPH

OF

NORTH AMERICAN BATS.

FAM. MEGADERMATIDÆ.

MACROTUS, GRAY.

Macrotus, GRAY, Pr. Zool. Soc. 1843, 21.

Ears large, joined; leafy appendage simple, erect; interfemoral membranes large; point of tail free.

Fig. 1.

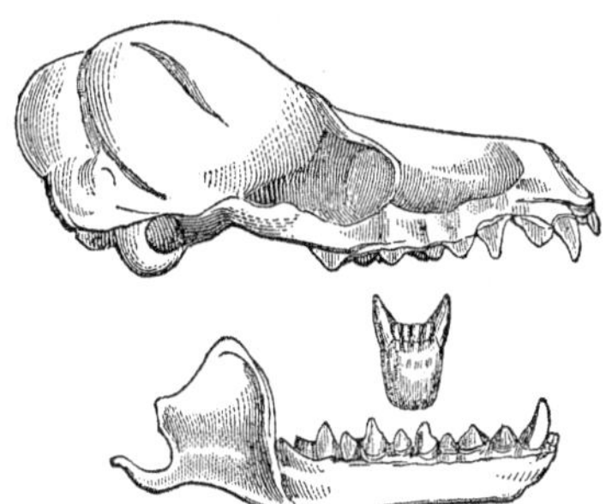

Macrotus californicus.

Skull thin, light, tapering. The cranium inflated; parietal crest small.

Dentition.

Molars $\frac{5}{6}$. Canines $\frac{1}{1}$. Incisors $\frac{4}{4}$. Canines $\frac{1}{1}$. Molars $\frac{5}{6}$ = 34 teeth.

Upper Jaw.—The incisors disproportionate; the central large and chisel-shaped; the lateral small, pointed, and converging. Canines small, slightly concave on inner, convex on outer surface;

no basal cusps. First premolar of peculiar shape, thin and compressed. It is unicuspid, with a small posterior basal point visible from without. The second is thicker, and has an internal basal ridge. The third and fourth molars not peculiar. The fifth is small, greatly compressed from within outwards.

Lower Jaw.—Incisors crowded, indistinctly trilobed; canines with a marked basal cusp. The first and second premolars of about equal size, thick, with basal ridge. The remaining molars not peculiar.

In placing this genus under *Megadermatidæ* it should not be considered as having any strong affinity to the genus *Megaderma*. When a family or subfamily is extensive, the first and last members of it often differ considerably from one another; and in the present instance the genus *Megaderma* may be considered to stand at one end of the subfamily, while *Macrotus* is at the other, the intervening members being wanting.

The nose leaf of *Megaderma* is complex and naked, that of *Macrotus* is simple and hairy. *Megaderma* has no tail, while that of *Macrotus* is produced beyond the interfemoral membrane. *Macrotus* has some resemblance to that group of *Phyllostomatidæ*, of which *Glossophaga* is the type. The head has the same long, rostroid appearance, the small acuminated nose leaf, the cleft in the lower lip, and the abrupt interfemoral membrane. The genus, in fact, appears to stand between *Megadermatidæ* and *Phyllostomatidæ*.

The genus *Macrotus* was established by Gray in the Proc. Zool. Soc. for 1843, p. 21, upon specimens of *M. waterhousii* brought from Hayti by Dr. Parnell. The description was very brief, and accompanied by no mention of the dentition.

Macrotus californicus, Baird.

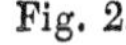

Fig. 2.

Fig. 3.

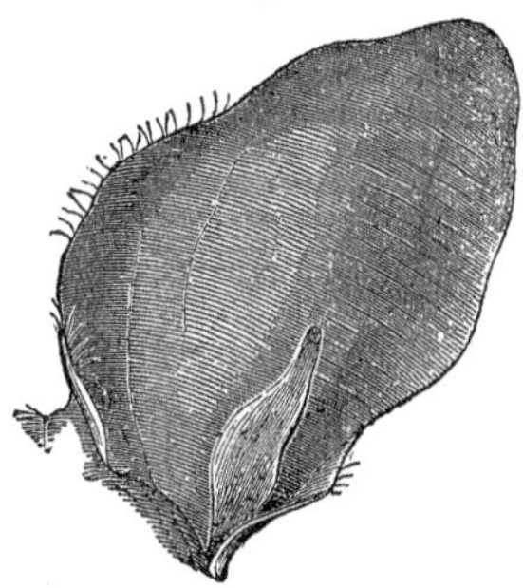

Macrotus californicus, Baird, Proc. Acad. Nat. Sc. Phila. 1858, 117.—Ib. Rep. U. S. and Mex. Bound. Surv. II, 1859, Mammals, p. 4, pl. i, fig. 2.

Description.—Head long. Face hairy. Eyes rather large, almond-shaped. Nose leaf acuminate, higher than broad, its narrow nostrils placed in its base obliquely. Ears very large, united over the head by an incised, transverse membrane; they are oval and slightly hairy. Tragus not quite half as high as the auricle; lanceolate straight on outer border, where at base there is an abrupt increase in width with a slight revolution posteriorly; inner border not thickened, the upper half concave, lower half convex. Lower lip cleft, shield triangular acute. Thumb slender, long; basal joint shortest. Tail produced two lines beyond the interfemoral membrane. The calcaneum large. Wing membrane extends to ankle; in some specimens it seems to arise by a slight attachment from the calcaneum in the same manner as in the genus *Natalus*. Foot moderate, with short compressed hairs on upper surface, claws rather large.

The fur is indistinctly tricolored. Above, base white, terminal third fawn, its tip gray. Below, base likewise white, terminal third fawn, its tip white—thus giving the fur a grizzled, wavy appearance. The hair about the face is shorter and more inclined to brown. Immediately behind the junction of the ears the head is almost naked. The basal portions of the ears have growths of hair upon them which may be contiguous in the living animal.

This species is closely related to *M. waterhousii*, Gray, of Cuba, Hayti, and other West Indian Islands; but a comparison of the type with good specimens of the latter from Cuba, preserved in alcohol, and presented by Prof. Poey to the Smithsonian Institution, show unmistakable differences, as do others from Jamaica, recently received from Mr. March.

The chin plates are less acutely defined ; the internal border of the tragus is much thickened, and the revoluted portion at the base of the external border is slightly swollen. The fur is bicolored ; central portion dark-brown instead of fawn. The nose leaf is of about the same height as in the above species ; the tail, however, is .25 of an inch shorter. The dentition is similar.

The *M. mexicana*, Saussure, is a species from Mexico described by M. Saussure in Revue et Mag. de Zool., 2d series, XII, 1860, p. 486. The author states that the description is taken from a specimen which was in poor condition. It is difficult to tell from his description whether his species is the same as *M. californicus* or not.

Fig. 4.

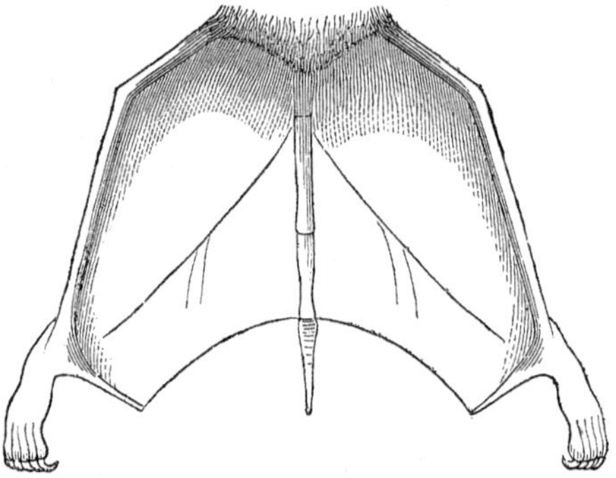

Macrotus californicus.

MEASUREMENTS.

Current number.	Original number.	From tip of nose to tail.	Length of tail.	Height of nose-leaf.	Length of forearm.	Length of tibia.	Length of longest finger.	Length of thumb.	Height of ear.	Height of tragus.	Expanse.	Nature of specimen.
2347		2.3	1.6	0.2	1.10	0.9	3.3	0.5	1.1	0.5	10.0	Alc.
5214	417	2.0	1.3	0.2	1.8	0.8	3.0	0 5	1.0	0.4½	10.0	"
5214*a*	411	2 0	1.4	0.2	1.10	0.10	3.2	0.4	1.2	0 5	10 0	"
5214*b*	410	2.0	1.3	0.2	2 0	0.10	3.0	0.5	1.0	0.4½	10.0	"
5214*c*	797	2.0	1.2	0.2	2 0	0 8	3.0	0.5	1.0	0.5	11 0	"
5214*d*		2.0	1.4	0.2	1.8	0 10	3.0	0.5	0.11	0 4	10.6	"
5214*e*	412	2.0	1.4	0.2	1.9	0.9	3.0	0.5	1.0	0 6	11.0	"
6174	415	2.0	1.3	0.2	1.8	0.8	3.0	0.5	1.0	0.5	10.6	"

LIST OF SPECIMENS.

Cat. No.	Specimens.	Locality.	Presented by	Nature of Spec'n.
2347	1	Fort Yuma, Cal.	Maj. G. H. Thomas.	In alcohol (type).
5214	28	Cape St. Lucas.	John Xantus.	In alcohol.
6174	1	Cape St. Lucas.	John Xantus.	In alcohol.

FAM. NOCTILIONIDÆ.

NYCTINOMUS, GEOFF.

Nyctinomus, ET. GEOFFROY, Desc. de l'Egypte (Hist. Nat.), II, 1814.—IS. GEOFFROY, Ann. des Sc. Nat. I, 1824, 337.—CASTELNAU, Exp. d'Amer. Sud; Mammif. pl. xii, f. 2.

Ears generally joined; lips thick, pendulous, grooved; nose sharp, well defined; tragus obtuse, broad and square; tail produced beyond the interfemoral membrane nearly half its length; great toes separated from the others, and fringed on their outer side.

Fig. 5.

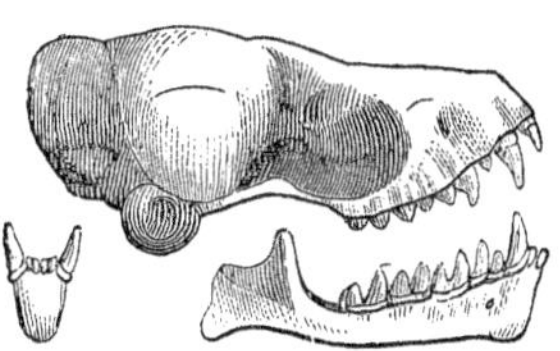

N. nasutus.

Skull.—The cranium is inflated, with no appearance of crest, and very papery. The anterior nares small. Intermaxillary bones rudimentary; facial angle small. Auditory capsules large. Lower jaw slender and elongated.

Dentition.

Molars $\frac{5}{5}$. Canines $\frac{1}{1}$. Incisors $\frac{2}{4}$. Canines $\frac{1}{1}$. Molars $\frac{5}{5}$=30 teeth.

Upper Jaw.—Superior incisors converge but do not touch. The first premolar is very small, but not hidden; the second has a sharp, well defined internal cusp. The internal cusp of the third upper molar has a posterior prolongation; last molar large.

Lower Jaw.—The incisors are very small, bilobed and crowded. The canines are slender, with an internal cusp, which does not meet its fellow in the middle line. Two premolars of nearly equal size, unicuspid, the posterior being a little the larger. The remaining three molars are in nowise peculiar.

A singular confusion has always existed in the efforts of naturalists to accurately determine the forms of the Molossoid group of the Noctilionidæ.

The names of *Vespertilio, Molossus, Dysopes, Dinops* and *Nyctinomus*, have been applied almost indiscriminately to the different species. Geof. St. Hilaire established the genus *Molossus*, in 1805, in Ann. du Mus. VI, 150. In 1814, he founded the genus *Nyctinomus* in the "Description de l'Egypte." As far as my observation has been extended, it is among these two genera that the different species can be properly grouped, excepting perhaps the form *Cheiromeles*, Horsf. *Molossus* is an American genus. *Nyctinomus* has an extensive distribution, being found in Africa, Australia, and America. Peters, in "Reise nach Mozambique," has described two African species under the names of *Dysopes brachypterus* and *limbatus*, but the figured skulls and heads correspond exactly to those of *Nyctinomus*. Tomes, while adverse to the separation, states that if separated, *Molossus australis*, Gould, from Australia, belongs to *Nyctinomus*. Horsfield's elaborate and sagacious researches in Asia have brought to light *N. tenuis;* and finally, Is. St. Hilaire noticed as early as 1824 (Ann. des Sc. Nat., April, 1824), the prevalence of the genus in America.

Nyctinomus can readily be distinguished from *Molossus* by the following characters:—

Molossus. Superior incisors converge and touch. Molars four in upper jaw; internal cusp of third molar not prolonged posteriorly; last molar small. Skull not markedly broad. Lips thick and heavy, but not furrowed. Nose rounded. Tragus a mere point of integument.

Nyctinomus. Superior incisors converge but do not touch. Molars in upper jaw five; internal cusp of third upper molar having a posterior prolongation; last molar large. Skull broad. Lips very pendulous and furrowed. Nose sharp, well defined. Tragus obtuse, broad, and square.

Nyctinomus nasutus, Tomes.

Fig. 6.

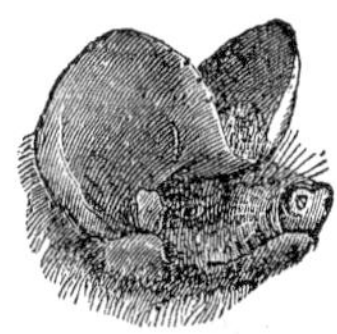

Fig. 7.

Molossus nasutus, Spix, Sim. et Vesp. Bras., 1823, 60, pl. xxxv, fig. 7; *fide* Isis, August, 1824, 899 (Brazil).—Schinz, Syn. Mamm. I, 1844, 143.

Dysopes nasutus, Temm., Mon. Mamm. I, 1827, 234.—Ib. Zool. Jour. III, 1828, 459.—Wagner, Suppl. Schreber, I, 1844, 474.—Ib. V, 1855, 711.

Nyctinomus nasutus, Tomes, Pr. Zool. Soc. Lond. 1861, 68 (Jamaica).

Nyctinomus brasiliensis, Isid. Geoff., Ann. des Sc. Nat. I, April, 1824, 337, pl. xxii (Brazil).—Ib. Zool. Journ. I, 1825, 133.—Ferussac, Bull. des Sc. Nat. II, 1824, 74.

Nyctinomus murinus, Gray, Griffith's Cuv. Ann. Kingdom, V, 1828, 66.

Nycticea cynocephala, Leconte, Cuv. An. Kingdom (McMurtrie) I, 1831, 432 (South Carolina).

Molossus cynocephalus, Cooper, Ann. N. Y. Lyc. IV, 1837, 65, pl. iii, fig. 1.—Wagner, Suppl. Schreber, V, 1855, 714.

Molossus fuliginosus, Cooper, Ann. N. Y. Lyc. IV, 1837, 67, pl. iii, f. 3 (S. Carolina.)

Rhinopoma carolinensis, Gundlach, Archiv f. Natur. 1840, 358, (not of Geoff., in Desm. Mamm. 1820, 130, and Dict. d'Hist. Nat. XLV, 1829). —Leconte, Pr. A. N. Sc. Phil. VII, 1855, 437.

? *Dysopes naso*, Wagner, Suppl. Schreb. I. 1840, 475, based on *Nyctinomus brasiliensis*, Geoff.

Nyctinomus mexicanus, Sauss., Rev. et Mag. de Zool. XI, 1860, 283.

Description.—Head rather large; made to appear more so by the heavy pendulous lips. Ears broad as high, obtusely square, almost joining on top of the head; on their inner anterior border five minute warts are observed. The outer border is emarginate at its upper, strongly concave at its lower portion, where at its basal third it is doubled upon itself. The mouth has upon it a bristled wart. The tragus is small, very obtuse; the outer border rather the longer. It is furnished at the tip with three or four bristles. The sides of the face are very little swollen. The inflated portions are continuous with the inner border of the ear, and both it and the pendulous lips, which are crimped into eight perpendicular lines, are studded with stiff bristles some three lines in length, those near the mouth being shorter. The snout is prominent, produced, truncated, and emarginate; a little ridge runs down the median line. The upper margin is beautifully crenulated, the lower is thickly set with a row of projecting setae, between which and the base of the nostrils runs a deep groove. The nostrils themselves are simple, rounded, and open sublaterally. The lower lips are thick but not crimped; they are quite bristly, and a small median wart is placed three lines from the mouth.

The fur is thick, short, soft, and almost entirely confined to the body. Above it is dark fawn at tip, with a base of a whitish hue. It extends up upon the back of the ears one-third their height. There is a very delicate patch on the interbrachial membrane. In front the color is light cinereus at base; tip a delicate fawn. Thumb moderate. Foot large; toes furnished with long hairs; the first and fifth fingers with numerous and thicker hairs in addition.

Nyctinomus nasutus, Tomes, has been selected as the name of this species after careful search. For a long time, *N. brasiliensis*, Is'd. Geof., was thought to have the priority, but the reference following *Dysopes nasutus*, Spix, in the above synonymy, shows clearly that this description has the priority of one year over the former. Mr. Tomes's name follows the title, since he was the first to give it its proper name.

Geoff. St. Hilaire, after founding the genus *Nyctinomus*, is said to have described a bat from North America, which was called *Rhinopoma carolinensis*. This is considered by Major Leconte to be the same as the species under consideration. But *Nyctinomus* has a naked nose, while *Rhinopoma* has a well developed noseleaf and operculum. There has been no figure given of this animal, but a glance at a figure of another species of the same genus, *R. macrophylla*, Geoff., Plates of the "Description de l'Egypte," pl. i, fig. 1 (erroneously entitled *Taphozous filet*), will at once show the wide differences existing between *Rhinopoma* and *Nyctinomus*. I have discarded Geoffroy's name, therefore, thinking it very probable that it has had an erroneous locality thrust upon it.[1] It is somewhat singular that Major Leconte should have adopted this name at the sacrifice of his own—*Nycticea cynocephala*—upon the bare supposition that the specific name, *carolinensis*, might lead to the conclusion that *Rhinopoma* had been found in North America. As far as I have been enabled to observe, there are no leaf-nosed bats whatever inhabiting the Atlantic slope of the United States.

The species *M. cynocephalus* and *fuliginosus*, of Mr. Cooper, evidently refer to the same animal; the minute differences observed in the ears are due to the circumstance that Mr. Cooper's descriptions were taken from dried specimens.

There is no longer much doubt about the extensive distribution of this species. Mr. Tomes[2] has examined specimens from different South American localities, and he affirms that they are identical with those obtained from South Carolina. I have also examined a specimen from Hayti, and another from Buenos Ayres, both of which belong to the Mus. Comp. Zoology, Cambridge, and they appear to be precisely similar to the more northern individuals.

It may be proper to state that Wagner considers the *Molossus nasutus* of Spix to be different from *Nyctinomus brasiliensis* of Geoffrey (= *D. nasutus*, Temm.), and gives the name of *D. naso* to the latter species. Burmeister also applies the latter name to a species found about Buenos Ayres (Reise durch die La Plata Staaten, II, 1861, 392) and in Chile.

[1] "This (*N. nasutus*) has been supposed by Major Leconte and others to be the *R. carolinensis* of M. Geoffroy; but having examined the types of this species in the Paris Museum, I am enabled to state that this is not the case. The *R. carolinensis* is a small *Molossus* from West Africa and Bourbon (*M. acetabulosus* = *M. natalensis*)."—Tomes, Pr. Zool. Soc. 1861, p. 68.

[2] "I have received specimens from many localities in South America and have compared them with others from Central America, and with the types of *N. brasiliensis* in the Paris Museum; and again with specimens of *N. fuliginosus* from Charleston, S. C., whence they had been sent by Dr. Bachman, and I find them to be all one species."—Tomes, *loc. cit.*

Measurements.

Current number.	Original number.	From tip of nose to tail.	Length of tail.	Length of forearm.	Length of tibia.	Length of longest finger.	Length of thumb.	Height of ear.	Height of tragus.	Expanse.	Nature of specimen.
5253	..	2.6	1 3	1.7	0.6	3.0	0.4	0.7	0.2	11.0	Alcoholic.
5494	..	2.6	1.1	1.9	0.6	3.0	0.4	0.7	0.2	10.3	"
	..	2.6	1.0	1.7	0.6	3.2	0.4	0.6	0.2	10.0	"
5227	..	2.4	1 3	1.6	0.6	3.2	0.4½	0.6	0.2	9.9	"
5219	..	2.3	1.3	1.6	0.6	3.0	0.3	0.7	0.2	10.0	"
	..	2.3	1.2	1.7	0.6	3.0	0.3	0.7	0.2	10.6	"
	..	2.0	1.3	1.6	0 5	3.0	0.3	0.7	0.2	10.4	"
5225	..	2.2	1.2	1.6	0.6	3.0	0.3	0.7	0.2	10.3	"

List of Specimens.

Cat. No.	No. of Sp.	Locality.	Presented by	Nature of Specimen.
5475	1	Upper Rio Grande.	Dr. T. C. Henry.	Dry.
5473	1	El Paso.	J. H. Clark.	"
5225	1	Eastern Texas.	" "	Alcoholic.
5219	3	Pecos to R. Grande.	Capt. J. Pope.	"
5496	2	Grand Coteau, La.	St. Chas. Coll.	"
5223	1	Matamoras.	Lt. Couch.	"
5227	1	Fort Yuma, Cal.	Maj. G. H. Thomas.	"
4742	1	"U. S."	Maj. Leconte.	Dry.

Fig. 8.

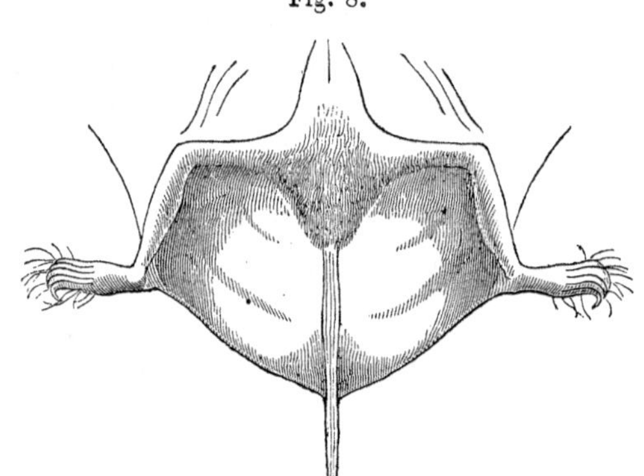

FAM. VESPERTILIONIDÆ.

NYCTICEJUS, RAF.

Nycticejus, RAF., Journal de Physique, LXXXVIII, 1819, 417.

Head short, broad, flat; ears small, simple, widely separated; upper incisors two; membranes naked.

Fig. 9.

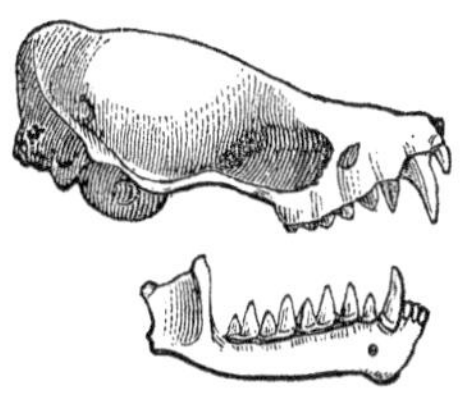

N. crepuscularis.

Skull.—Intermediate between that of *Scotophilus* and that of *Lasiurus*, flat, but not to the extent seen in the former; cranium inflated, but not so much as in the latter. It is not elevated; the occipital elevation is not abrupt. Compared with that of *L. noveboracensis*, a bat of nearly the same size, it is longer, and face more pointed. The palate is more level and does not slope so much at its posterior part. The infraorbital foramen is larger, with a slight tendency toward the formation of a groove. The lower jaw is less abrupt; the incisors are placed more anteriorly to the canines in a larger arc.

Dentition.

Molars $\frac{4}{5}$. Canines $\frac{1}{1}$. Incisors $\frac{2}{6}$. Canines $\frac{1}{1}$. Molars $\frac{4}{5}=30$ teeth.

Upper Jaw.—Incisors small, contiguous to canines, and slightly converging; canines large, simple. Molars not peculiar. The first more slender and longer than the others, but not so broad; destitute of the W-shaped crown.

Lower Jaw.—Incisors not crowded, bifid. Canine simple, turned markedly backward; basal ridge anteriorly well developed; first premolar larger than the same tooth in *Lasiurus*, but in comparison with the second is of itself small. The second premolar, if produced, would not touch an extended line from the canine. The basal ridges of both these teeth are large. Molars proper, not peculiar.

This genus of Rafinesque's has until recently held an uncertain position. As imperfectly defined by its describer the presence of two incisors only, in the upper jaw, was brought out as the prominent generic characteristic. But, as it was afterwards observed, the incisors are variable, the young, it was thought, having four incisors, the adult but two. And even this observation applied more to the genus as then understood than to it as now restricted; for the above fact in relation to the dentition is also observed in *L. noveboracensis*. So we conclude that the presence of but two incisors in the upper jaw of *Nycticejus* is still a permanent character, though not a very important one.

Nycticejus crepuscularis, Allen.

Fig. 10.

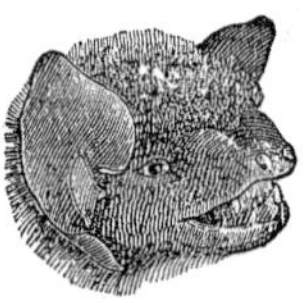

Fig. 11.

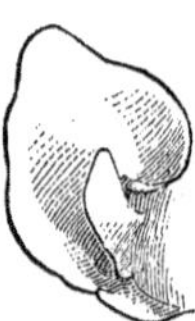

Vespertilio crepuscularis, Lec., Cuv. An. Kingdom (McMurtrie ed.), I, 1831, 432.—Ib., Proc. Acad. Nat. Sci. VII, 1855, 433.
Vespertilio creeks, Fr. Cuv. Nouv. Ann. du Mus. I, 1832, 18.
Nycticejus humeralis, (?) Raf., Journal de Physique, LXXXVIII, 1819, 417.

Description.—Ears small, internal basal lobe small and curved; the external basal lobe also rather inconspicuous; between the latter and the angle of the mouth a small wart is present. Tragus straight on internal, irregularly convex on outer border. Face black; nostrils simple, not produced, very little emarginated; sides of face much swollen. Lower jaw has a rather large naked space at chin. Eyes small, with a wart above on either side. Thumb moderate. Membranes blackish-brown, extending to base of toes. Feet rather small, slightly haired above. Interfemoral triangular, moderately ample. Calcaneum slight. Tip of tail exserted.

The general expression is thus observed to be that of *Scotophilus*, but it differs from that genus in the blackish hue of the membranes of ear and skin of face, and in the smallness of the former.

The fur is rather scanty, with the exception of a small patch at base of the interfemoral membrane; before and behind there is no hair on the membranes. The lower third of posterior surface of ears is covered with soft hair. The fur is inclined to be woolly; everywhere it is rather short. That of the back is dark fawn for the upper half, the lower half being a lighter hue bordering on brown. In front the color is more uniform and lighter, being plumbeous at base, light brown at tips. In one specimen, No. 882, Georgia, Phila. Acad., the fur runs on to the membranes before and behind midway to the elbow. In another, No. 283, Carlisle, Pa., the coloration in front resembles *V. subulatus*, Say, that of the back more brownish.

MEASUREMENTS.

Current number.	Original number.	From tip of nose to tail.	Length of tail.	Length of forearm.	Length of tibia.	Length of longest finger.	Length of thumb.	Height of ear.	Height of tragus.	Expanse.	Nature of specimen.
5312	..	2.0	1.5	1.4	0.6	2.6	0.4	0 4	0.2½	9 6	Alcoholic.
	..	2 0	1.5	1.4	0.6	2.6	0.4	0.5	0.2	9.9	"
	..	2.0	1.5	1.4	0.6	2 5	0.3	0.4	0.3	9.3	"
5313	..	2.0	1.4½	1.4	0.6	2.6	0.3	0.4	0.3	9.3	"
5322	..		1.5	1.4	0.6	2.6½	0.4	0.5	0.3		"
5329	..	2.0	1.2	1.3	0.6	2.3½	0.4	0.4	0.2½	9.3	"
	..	2.0	1.2	1.6	0.6	2.7	0.4	0.4½	0.2½	9.9	"
4735	..	2 0	1.2	1.3	0.6	2.5	0.4	0 4	0 2	8.6	Dry.
4736	..	2.0	1.2	1.3	0.6	2.1	0.3	0.3½	0.2	7.9	"
111	..	1.6				2.2	0.3	0.4	0.2		"
283	..	1.9	1.4	1.4	0.6	2.2	0 3	0.4	0.2½	7.6	"
882	..	2.0	1.3	1.5	0.6	2.4	0.3	0.6½	0.3	8.0	"

LIST OF SPECIMENS.

Cat. No.	No. of Sp.	Locality.	Presented by	Nature of Spec'm.
5448	1	Carlisle, Pa.	S. F. Baird.	Dry.
5350	1	Washington, D. C.	?	Alcoholic.
5312	2	Liberty Co., Ga.	Dr. Jos. Jones.	"
5313	1	New Orleans.	N. O. Academy.	"
5300	1	St. Louis, Mo.	Dr. G. Engelmann.	"
5322	1	Nebraska.	Dr. Cooper.	"
5397	1	Redmond's Ranch, Tex.	J. H. Clark.	"
5372	3	Matamoras, (Berl. Col.).	Lt. D. N. Couch.	"
5329	2	" "	" "	"
4736	1	"U. S."	Maj. Leconte.	Dry.
5539	1	?	?	"

LASIURUS, RAF. (?)

Head depressed, lips slightly fringed; nostrils wide apart; skull flat, massive; occipital crest prominent.

Fig. 12.

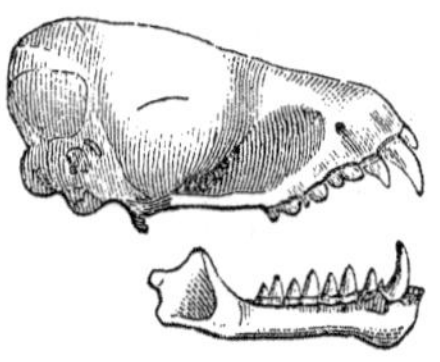

Lasiurus noveboracensis.

Skull broad, high, sub-angular; facial line abruptly elevated; marked depressions in the facial bones in the median line; zygomas complete.

Dentition.

Molars $\frac{5}{5}$ or $\frac{4}{5}$. Can. $\frac{1}{1}$. Inc. $\frac{2}{6}$. Can. $\frac{1}{1}$. Mol. $\frac{5}{5}$ or $\frac{4}{5}$ = 32 or 30 teeth.

Superior incisors stout, placed close beside the canines.

In the young animals the number of incisors in the upper jaw, four.

The name, *Lasiurus*, it has been asserted, was first applied to a genus of *Vespertilionidæ* by Rafinesque. Dr. Gray,[1] quoting this author, adopts the name but without defining the genus. Mr. Tomes, in his Monograph of *Lasiurus*,[2] while dwelling at length on the species, says nothing of the characters common to them all, nor have I been able to find in any author the desired information as to who gave the original description and where its record is to be found. It appears, nevertheless, that naturalists have readily recognized the propriety of considering *Lasiurus* as distinct from *Vespertilio*.

The following is a synopsis of the species included under *Lasiurus* :—

a. Posterior surface of interfemoral membrane concealed by hair.
- Border of ear light brown . . . . . *L. noveboracensis.*
- Border of ear black . . . . . . *L. cinereus.*

b. Posterior surface of interfemoral membrane exposed. *L. intermedius.*

Lasiurus noveboracensis, TOMES.

The Red Bat.

Fig. 13.

Fig. 14.

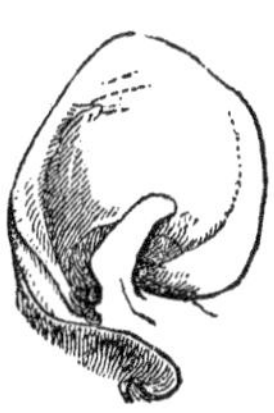

Vespertilio noveboracensis, ERXL. Syst. Reg. Anim. 1777, 135.—HARLAN, Fauna Amer. 1825, 20.—GODMAN, Amer. Nat. Hist. I, 1826, 50.—COOPER, Ann. Lyc. Nat. Hist. N. Y. 1837, 57.—DEKAY, Nat. Hist. N. Y. (Zool.) 1842, 6, pl. ii.—LECONTE, Proc. Acad. Nat. Sci. 1855, 432.

Nycticejus noveboracensis, LECONTE, Cuv. Regn. Anim. (McMurtrie's) Ap-

---

[1] List of the species of Mammalia of the British Museum, 1843, 32.

[2] Proc. Zool. Soc. XXV, 1857, 34.

pendix, 1831, 432.—TEMM. Monog. II, 1835-1841, 158.—WAGNER, Suppl. Schreb. Säug. I, 1840, 546.—IB. V, 1855, 773.—SCHINZ, Synopsis Mam. I, 1844, 199.—MAX PRINCE WIED, Archiv Naturg. 1861, 188.

Lasiurus noveboracensis, TOMES, Proc. Zool. Soc. 1857, 34.

Vespertilio lasiurus, GMEL. Syst. Nat. 1788.—SCHREB. Säug. 1826.—GEOFF. Ann. du Mus. VIII, 1806, 200, f. 6.—DESM. Mam. 1820, 142.—FISCH. Synop. Mam. 1829, 109.

Nycticejus lasiurus, WAGNER, Schreb. Säug. Suppl. V, 1855, 772.

Vespertilio rubellus, PALISOT DE BEAUVOIS, Cat. Peale's Mus. 1796.

Vespertilio villosissimus, GEOFF. Ann. du Mus. VIII, 1806, 478.—DESM. Mam. 1830, 143.—FISCH. Syn. Mam. 1829, 110.—RENGG. Säugt. von Parag. 1830, 83.—WAGNER, Supp. Schreb. Säug. I, 1840, 536.

Vespertilio monachus, RAF. Am. Month. Mag. IV, 1817, 445.

Vespertilio tessalatus, IB.

Taphyzous rufus, HARLAN, Fauna Americana, 1825, 23.

Vespertilio rufus, WARDEN, Descript. United States, V, 602. (?)

Lasiurus rufus, GRAY, List. Mam. Brit. Mus. 1843, 32.—GOSSE, Naturalist in Jamaica, 1851, 280.

Vespertilio blossevillii, LESS. et GARN. Bull. des Sci. Nat. VIII, 95.—FISCH. Synop. Mam. 1829, 110.—LA SAGRA, Hist. de l'Ile de Cuba, 1840, 6, pl. i, f. 4, 5, 6, 7, 8.

Vespertilio bonariensis, LESS. Voy. de la Coquille, 1829.

Nycticejus varius, POEPP. Reise Chili, I, 1835, 451.—WAGNER, Suppl. Schreb. Säugt. I, 1840, 547.—GAY, Hist. de Chili, (Zool.) I, 1848, 37.

New York Bat, PENN. Syn. Quad. 1771, 367.—PENN. Arct. Zool. 1792, 184. —KIRTLAND, Zöol. Report, 175.—EMMONS, Mass. Report, 1840, 9.

Red Bat, Wilson Ornith. VI, 50, f. 4.

Habitat.—Universally distributed throughout the temperate regions of North America; moderately abundant.

Description.—Head and face hairy; nose blunt, rounded, slightly emarginated; nostrils opening semi-laterally. The sides of the face slightly inflated and set with small stiff hairs. A similar row of longer hair surrounds the eyes. The upper lip, especially at the sides of the face, is more massive than the lower, and is somewhat produced. The ears are sub-rounded;—the inner border straight until near the tip where it suddenly turns outwards;—at its base is a well developed lobe which lies close to, but slightly behind the tragus. The outer border is slightly convex, and terminates at the angle of the mouth. On a line with the outer border of the ear a sharply defined lobe is noticed, which at first appears to be the termination of the border, but upon close examination it is found to continue on to the angle of the mouth. Between this lobe and the mouth there is placed a small wart which is covered with setæ. The tragus is half the height of the ear, is straight on the inner edge, except at the point, where it turns abruptly inwards. The outer border has a very irregular outline. The basal portion is indentated. This indentation, which, in comparison to other species of *Vespertilionidæ* is considerable, is of itself not very deep, and ends in the most convex point of the tragus, whence the border runs upward and inward to the tip. The lower jaw is covered with short hairs, and has at its symphysis a small naked space which is gradually lost along the sides of the mouth. The posterior surface of the ear is covered with hair one-half its length, which extends upon the anterior production of the external border down to the angle of the mouth.

The fur of the body is everywhere long and silky. Anteriorly it is rather denser though not quite so long as that posteriorly. It is of a light russet red, tinged with yellow—being tipped with gray toward the neck, and verging to a fawn color, in some specimens, towards the pubis. Fur of the same general hue extends from the body upon the alar membranes up to the base of the third finger of either side and blends with that upon the anterior surface of the interfemoral membrane at about the region of the tibio-femoral articulation. The hair upon the latter membrane runs down fully one-half its length in most specimens. The interbrachial expansion also possesses a sparse growth of yellowish fur. Posteriorly the fur is very long and presents a richer appearance than anteriorly. The russet red color is here predominant in the majority of individuals, though we meet with a great variety of hues of fawn, fawn-red, and yellowish cinereous. At each shoulder a conspicuous white tuft of hair is seen; this is not elevated above the surrounding fur of the neck with which its whitish color gradually blends.

The posterior surface of the alar membranes is less extensively furred along the brachial and digital regions than the anterior surface, being here almost altogether confined to longitudinal bands extending from the neck downwards across the interbrachial membrane midway from the shoulder to the elbow, and thence continuing along the sides of the body and external border of the tibia to the ankle and tarsus of either side. The dorsum of the fifth finger, for about one-third of its length, is covered with fine scattering hair, which in some individuals is not confined thereto but extends between the fourth and fifth fingers. The basal joint of the thumb is decorated with a whitish tuft. The posterior surface of the interfemoral is very thickly covered over its whole area with fur of the same color as that of the body.

The difference in hue of the various individuals is chiefly owing to the coloration of the tips of the hair. Each hair is tinged as follows:—

The base dark plumbeous in color, verging to black; the centre, a delicate yellowish-brown, passing onwards toward the tip to a darkish red, in some instances to a brighter red, more rarely to a beautiful chocolate. The point is generally white. The grayish chocolate and dark red varieties are the principal ones seen in the northern specimens, while the bright red prevails among those of warmer sections of the country.

The hair covering the interfemoral membrane before and behind is indistinctly bi-colored; the irregular growths scattered elsewhere upon the alar membranes are unicolored.

The color of the membranes is a rich brown, bordering on a yellowish-brown, about the head. The ears and lips are marked with yellow in the same manner as in the next species (*L. cinereus*) they are marked with black.

Fig. 15.

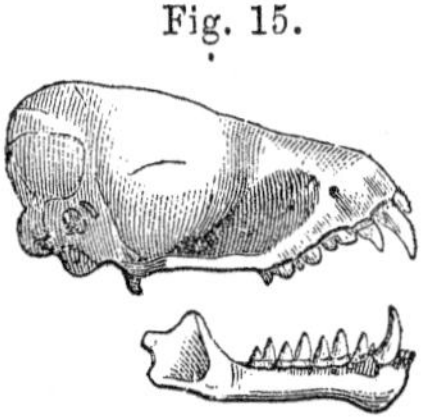

Fig. 16.

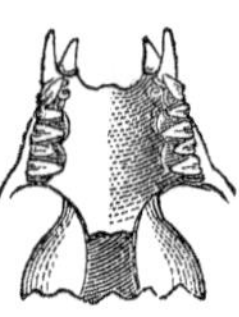

Skull small; occiput high; cranium broad.

Dentition.

Molars $\frac{5}{5}$. Canines $\frac{1}{1}$. Incisors $\frac{2}{6}$. Canines $\frac{1}{1}$. Molars $\frac{5}{5}$ = 32 teeth.

Upper Jaw.—Incisors small, strongly convergent; canines simple. First premolar very minute, entirely hidden from view externally by the close position of the second premolar to the canine; molars not peculiar except the last, which is small and thin, compressed from before backwards.

Lower Jaw.—Incisors crowded; canines pointing backwards.

First and second premolars distinct; first smaller than second, which leans toward the canine, and its axis, if produced, would touch it. Other molars as usual.

I regret that my material will not allow me to decide the interesting question whether this species really occurs in South America. My most southern specimens come from the Rio Grande, Texas, and Cape St. Lucas—no difference being observed between them and the more northern individuals.

Dr. J. E. Gray (Zool. Proc., 1862, 143) gives a notice of a Lasiurian bat from the Sandwich Islands which he asserts to be the *L. Grayii*, Tomes. This fact is of interest, since it proves that the same species may have a distribution from the Sandwich Islands to Chili, where Mr. Tomes' specimen was collected.

According to Dr. Gray, *loc. cit.*, there is a specimen labelled *L. Grayii*, Tomes, in the British Museum, from Nisqually, Straits of Juan de Fuca. I have, however, never met with any bat in North America answering to Mr. Tomes' description.

Fig. 17.

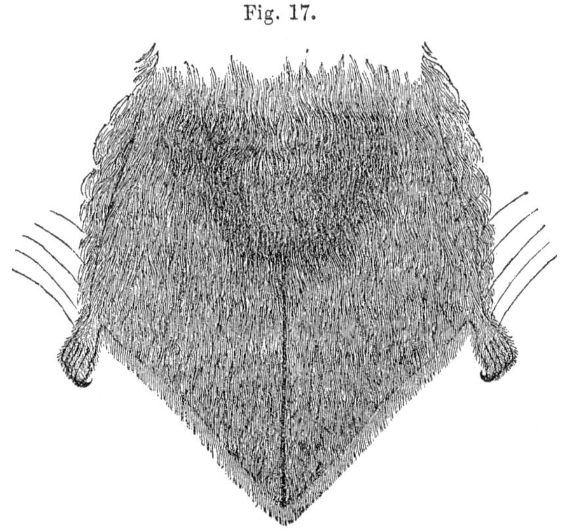

MEASUREMENTS.

Current number.	Original number.	From tip of nose to tail.	Length of tail.	Length of forearm.	Length of tibia.	Length of longest finger.	Length of thumb.	Height of ear.	Height of tragus.	Expanse.	Nature of specimen.
5266	..	1.9	2.0	1.6	0.9	3.3	0.4½	0.4	0.2	10.9	
5267	..	1.9	2.0	1.6	0.9	3.5	0.4½	0.6	0.3	12.0	
67	..	2.0	1.9	1.6	0.9	3.0	0.4	0.5	0.3	11.6	
..	..	2.0	1.9	1.6	0.9	3.5	0.4½	0.4	0.3	12.0	
..	..	2.0	1.9	1.5	0.9	2.9	0.4	0.5	0.3	11.0	
..	..	2.0	1.9	1.6	0.9	3.0	0.4½	0.4	0.3	11.0	

LIST OF SPECIMENS.

Cat. No.	Specimens.	Locality.	Presented by	Nature of Spec'n.
5242	1	Muskeeget Isl., Mass.	Dr. T. M. Brewer.	In alcohol.
5243	2	Wethersfield, Conn.	Charles Wright.	"
5245	2	Mt. Holly, N. J.	Dr. Brown.	"
6188–90	3	Carlisle, Pa.	S. F. Baird.	"
5244	17	Carlisle, Pa.	S. F. Baird.	"
5540	2	Ann Arundel Co., Md.	J. H. Clark.	"
5247–8	2	Washington, D. C.	National Institute.	"
5246	1	Washington, D. C.	Dr. Nichols.	"
5257	8	Columbus, Ga.	Dr. Gesner.	"
5256	5	Liberty Co., Ga.	Dr. W. L. Jones.	"
5263	1	Tallahassee, Fla.	T. Glover.	"
5314	1	Micanopy, Fla.	Dr. J. B. Bean.	"
5260	2	Eutaw, Ala.	Prof. Winchell.	"
5259	1	Washington, Miss.	Col. B. L. C. Wailes.	"
5252	1	Washington, Miss.	Col. B. L. C. Wailes.	"
5253	1	Monticello, Miss.	Miss H. Tennison.	"
5464	1	Columbus, Miss.	Dr. Spillman.	Dry skin.
5261	2	Tyree Springs, Tenn.	Prof. R. Owen.	In alcohol.
5262	2	Knoxville, Tenn.	Prof. Mitchell.	"
5274	1	Grand Coteau, La.	St. Charles College.	"
5270	1	Prairie Mer Rouge, La.	James Fairie. [U.S.A.	"
5253	1	Ft. Towson, Ark.	Dr. L. A. Edwards,	"
5254	2	Ft. Smith, Ark.	Dr. G. C. Shumard.	"
5256	3	Red River, Ark. ?	?	"
5251	1	Cass Co., Mo.	Dr. P. R Hoy.	"
5463	1	Missouri.	Dr. P. R. Hoy.	Dry skin.
5250	14	St. Louis, Mo.	Dr. G. Engelmann.	In alcohol.
4215	1	Neosho Falls, Kansas.	B. F. Goss.	Dry skin.
5249	6	Illinois.	R. Kennicott.	"
5460	1	Cook Co., Ill.	R. Kennicott.	"
5457	1	Racine, Wis.	Dr. P. R. Hoy.	"
5459	1	Albion, Mich.	R. R. Child.	"
5456	1	Grosse Isl., Mich.	Rev. Charles Fox.	"
5466	1	Lake Superior.	?	"
5458	1	Yellow Stone River.	Dr. F. V. Hayden.	"
5461	1	Yellow Stone River.	Col. Vaughan.	In alcohol.
5265	1	Nebraska.	Dr. J. G. Cooper.	"
5264	1	Laramie Peak, Neb.	Dr. Hayden.	"
5278	1	Cimarron River, Kans.	J. H. Clark.	"
5269	1	Pecos River, Tex.	Capt. J. Pope.	"
5272	3	Bet. Laredo & Camargo,	Arthur Schott.	"
5277	5	Matamoras. [Tex.	Lt. Couch. (Berl. Col.)	"
5268	1	Fort Bliss, N. Mex.	Do. S. W. Crawford.	"
5266	1	Fort Tejon, Cal.	John Xantus.	"
5267	1	Cape St. Lucas.	John Xantus.	"
5273	1	Rock Creek?	W. S. Wood.	"
5279	1	Locality unknown.	?	"
5275	1	" "	?	"
6185–7	3	" "	?	"
5271	1	" "	?	"
5541	1	" "	W. L. Le Duc.	"
				"

Lasiurus cinereus, Allen.

The Hoary Bat.

Fig. 18.

Fig. 19.

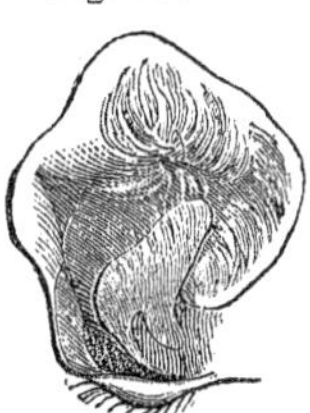

Vespertilio cinereus, Palisot de Beauvois, Cat. Peale's Mus. Phila. 1796, 14.—Leconte, Proc. Phila. Acad. Nat. Sci. 1855, 433.
Vespertilio pruinosus, Say, Long's Exp. to Rky. Mts. 1823, 67.—Harlan, Fauna Amer. 1825, 21.—Ib., Med. and Phys. Researches, 1831, 28.—Godman, Amer. Nat. Hist. 1826, 68, pl. ii, f. 3.—Richardson, Fauna Bor. Amer. 1829, 1.—Cooper, Ann. Lyc. N. York, IV, 1837, 54.—DeKay, Nat. Hist. N. York (Zool.), 1842, 7, pl. ii, f. 2.
Scotophilus pruinosus, Gray, Mag. Zool. and Bot. II, 1838, 498.
Nycticejus pruinosus, Temm. Monog. Mam. 1835, 154.—Wagner's Schreb. Säug. (Suppl.) I, 1840, 544.—Ib. V, 1855, 770.—Schinz, Syn. Mam. I, 1845, 197.—Max Pr. Wied, Archiv Naturg. 1861, 185.
Lasiurus pruinosus, Tomes, Proc. Zool. Soc. Lond. 1857, 37.

Description.—Head large, flat and hairy. Sides of the face somewhat inflated, the tips slightly whiskered. Nostrils wide apart, snout rather high, emarginated. Lower lip with smooth, naked space anteriorly. Ears broad as high, of a roundish form with large internal lobe, which lies close to the head and nearly covering the eyes and approaching closely the external inferior lobe. The internal border is markedly convex: in some specimens slightly emarginate at its tip—the external border being thinner than the internal, less convex and somewhat irregular in outline. The basal external lobe is very conspicuous and abrupt, with obtuse summit, and terminates on a line with the posterior angle of the eye. The tragus is broad, inner border straight; tip blunt, curved inwards; external border longer than internal, convex, upper two thirds convex the lower. The ears are black on the borders, rather extensively haired without, to a less extent within—the extreme border being naked. The tragus is slightly haired in front.

The fur is everywhere soft and thick; anteriorly less thick than posteriorly, and tinged as follows: neck, beneath the ears and lower jaw, of a faded yellow color; the breast of a dark fawn, tipped conspicuously with white—a mixture of these two colors, producing a dirty cinereous tinge towards the axillæ. The abdomen is of a more uniform color, the fawn hue predominating over the cinereous. Posteriorly the fur is longer, more luxuriant and variegated. The head and posterior surface of the ears are of the same yellowish hue as the anterior portion of neck. Below these points the hair is everywhere of a rich brownish chocolate, or umber smoky fawn color, tipped with white. This contrast of color gives the animal a very brilliant appearance, and has suggested for it the name of "hoary bat," by which it is generally known.

The fur upon the membranes has a distribution similar to that in *L. noveboracensis*. Anteriorly it extends in a wide band to the third finger upon the interbrachial membrane, and covers in one-third of the surface of the interfemoral membrane. Posteriorly this membrane, together with the dorsum of the foot, is entirely haired. The fur has not generally an extensive distribution upon the wing membranes, though in not a few individuals I have found this tendency marked. A small patch of fur is seen at the base of the thumb and fifth finger.

Each hair upon the body has four colors, with the exception of the regions about the head and belly where it has but two. The coloration is as follows: Base plumbeous black; next to this a dingy yellowish-brown; sub-tip is of the same hue as base; the tip being pure white.

The proportion of the basal color and the white tip is constant, but the other shades are variable. Thus upon the back of the neck is the light yellowish shade above mentioned, while the proportion of the plumbeous is scarcely noticeable. But the latter color gradually increases while the former decreases as the fur extends downwards until upon the loins the preponderance of the darker shade with an intermingling of umber brown is very marked. Upon the interfemoral membrane, posteriorly, the fur partakes of the same hue, tipped with grayish-white; that anteriorly has a fawn colored base with lighter tips.

The shoulder tuft is inconspicuous; on the membrane above the elbow there is a small whitish spot of hair.

Membranes very ample. Thumb large. Foot moderate.

Fig. 20.

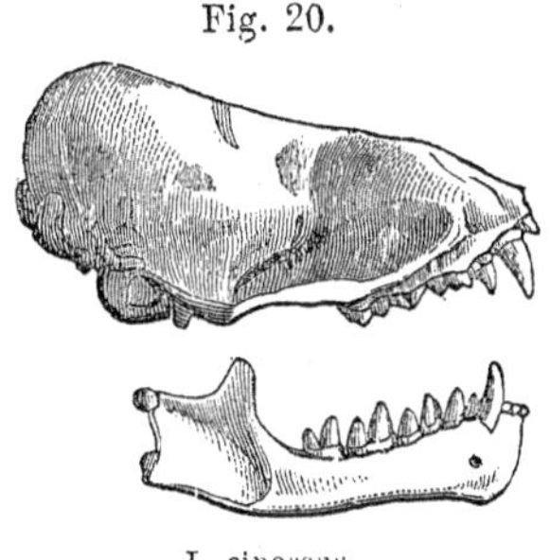

L. cinereus.

Skull.—Broad and high. Palate sloped considerably backwards.

Dentition.

Molars $\frac{5}{5}$. Canines $\frac{1}{1}$. Incisors $\frac{2}{6}$. Canines $\frac{1}{1}$. Molars $\frac{5}{5}$=32 teeth.

Upper Jaw.—Incisors stout, short, wide apart. Canines large and simple. First premolar very minute, wedged in between the canine and second premolar, which is large and pointed. Last molar compressed antero-posteriorly.

Lower Jaw.—Incisors bifid, but not much crowded. Canines with a small anterior cusp. Molars as usual, first smaller than second, which is not inclined so much anteriorly as in the preceeding species.

This species, since the date of Mr. Say's description, has generally been known as *V. pruinosus*, until Major Leconte claimed for M. Palisot de Beauvois the priority of the name *V. cinereus*, as described by him in the Catalogue of Peale's Mus., Phila., as early as 1796. This very rare pamphlet had evidently been overlooked by Mr. Say, and having been so fortunate as to find a copy in the library of the Phila. Academy I have no doubt that the description of Palisot de Beauvois is intended to apply to the species now under consideration.[1]

[1] See Appendix.

Dr. J. E. Gray, in Cat. of Mammalia, 1862, 49, has given Bolivia, S. A., as a locality for *L. cinereus*, but with perhaps insufficient authority.

MEASUREMENTS.

Current number.	Original number.	From tip of nose to tail.	Length of tail.	Length of forearm.	Length of tibia.	Length of longest finger.	Length of thumb.	Height of ear.	Height of tragus.	Expanse.	Nature of specimen.
5280	..	3.0	2.4	2.0	1.0	4.3	0.6	0.6	0.4	15.3	
14 (?)	..	3.0	2.5	2.2	1.0	4.1	0.7	0.6½	0.4	14.9	
147	..	2.6	1.8	2.0	0.11	4.0	0.6	0.4	0.3	13.4	
3255	..			2.0	1.0	4.1	0.6	0.4	0.3	12.6	
40	..	3.0	2.0	2.0	0.10	4.2	0.6	0.4	0.4	13.6	
4213	..	2.6	2.0	2.0	0.10	4.2	0.6			13.6	
4728	..			2.0	0.8	3.9	0.7	0.3½	0.3	11.6	
269	..	2.0	2.0	2.0	0.11	4.0	0.6	0.3	0.2½	12.6	
3098	..	2.0		2.0	0.10	4.0	0.7	0.4	0.2½		
1743	..	2.0	2.0	2.0	0.10	3.8	0.6	0.4	0.3	10.0	
73	..	2.6	2.0	2.0	0.12	4.0	0.6	0.4	0.3	12.0	
93	..	3.0		2.0	0.11	4.0	0.6		0.4	11.6	
873	..	2.6	2.0	2.0	0.11	4.0	0.6	0.4	0.3	12 6	
883	..	2.6	2.0	2.0	0.12	4.1	0.6	0.4	0.3	14.0	
415	..	2.6	2.0	2.0	0.10	4.0	0.6	0.4	0.3	14.0	

LIST OF SPECIMENS.

Cat. No.	No. of Sp.	Locality.	Presented by	Nature of Specimen.
5280	1	Halifax, N. S.	Dr. Gilpin.	Alcoholic.
6184	1	British America.	R. Kennicott.	"
5286	1	Red River settlem.	D. Gunn.	"
5417	1	Cleveland, O.	Dr. Kirtland.	Dry.
5421	1	Little Blue, Kansas.	W. S. Wood.	"
5281	2	St. Louis. Mo.	Dr. G. Engelmann.	Alcoholic.
5283	1	Grand Coteau, La.	St. Charles College.	"
5328	2	Ft. Pierre, Neb.	D. J. Evans.	"
5284	2	Near Ft. Union, Neb.	Dr. Hayden.	"
5422	1	Ft. Pierre, Neb.	" "	Dry.
4213	1	Neosho Falls, Kans.	B. F. Goss.	"
5415	1	South Fork Platte.	F. V. Hayden, M. D.	"
3768	1	La Boule River, Utah.	? [U. S. A. (?)	"
5414	1	Donana, N. M.	Dr. T. C. Henry,	"
5282	5	Matamoras.	Lt. Couch, Berl. Coll.	Alcoholic.
4728	1	"U. S."		Dry.
5286	2	Monterey, Cal.	A. S. Taylor.	Alcoholic.
5287	1	Petaluma, Cal.	E. Samuels.	"

Lasiurus intermedius, ALLEN.

Fig. 21.

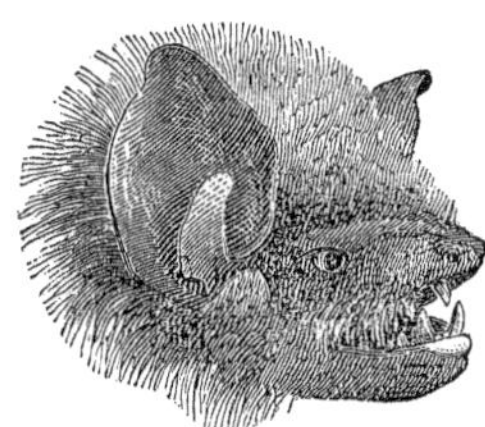

Fig. 22.

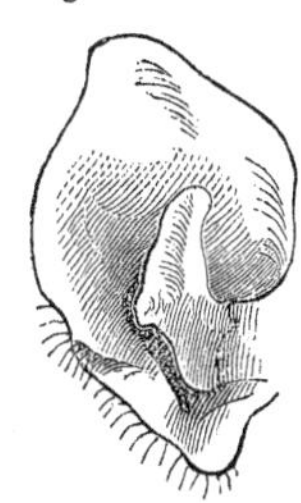

L. intermedius, ALLEN, Proc. Phila. Acad. Nat. Sciences, 1862, 146.

Description.—Head large, flat, hairy. Snout high, emarginate, and of a brown color. Nostrils opening sublaterally. Sides of face moderately inflated. Mouth and lower jaw fringed slightly with short hair. Small naked space at mentum. Ears high, elliptical, pointed, and nearly naked—strongly convex on their inner border, nearly straight on their outer—the lobe at the base of the outer border well developed. The tragus similar in shape to that of *L. cinereus*, but has a blunter incurved tip; it is slightly haired on facial surface. Eyes diminutive, placed near the ear. Thumb rather small. Feet moderate.

Fur not so extensive as in other species of the genus, posteriorly extending upon the wing membrane from body, as in *L. cinereus* —running down the interfemoral membrane but two-thirds the distance and on to the foot; a very small brownish tuft is seen at base of thumb, and on the membrane at and above the elbow, while the fourth and fifth fingers are naked. Anteriorly the hair spreads up under the arm to wrist as in other species, but less thickly. It also runs down a little way upon the interfemoral, and is observable upon the interbrachial membrane. The wing membrane extends to base of toes. The calcaneum is moderately developed.

General hue olive brown. Hairs blackish at base, dirty brown at centre, with a clearer tip. The color is somewhat darker behind than in front.

Dentition.

Molars $\frac{4}{5}$. Canines $\frac{1}{1}$. Incisors $\frac{2}{6}$. Canines $\frac{1}{1}$. Molars $\frac{4}{5}$ = 30 teeth.

The small premolar placed behind the canine of the upper jaw of *L. cinereus* and *L. noveboracensis* is here absent.

This species in size, physiognomy, number of incisors, and character of the distribution of the fur resembles the type of *Lasiurus*, while in shape of the ears and disposition of molars it is akin to *Scotophilus*. The interfemoral membrane is scarcely more hairy than in *S. noctivagans*, yet the entire contour of the animal is strongly Lasiurian. It is intermediate between *L. grayi*, Tomes, and *L. cinereus*, Pal. de Beauvois. It is larger than *L. grayi*, and smaller than the majority of specimens of *L. cinereus;* the thumb is small as in the former, but the wing membrane extends to the base of toes as in the latter; it is distinct from both in the brown fur, in the high ear and the scantiness of the hair on the interfemoral membrane.

MEASUREMENTS.

Current number.	Original number.	From tip of nose to tail.	Length of tail.	Length of forearm.	Length of tibia.	Length of longest finger.	Length of thumb.	Height of ear.	Height of tragus.	Expanse.	Nature of specimen.
5328	..	3.0	2 6	2 2	0.11	4.0	0.5	0.7½	0.3	13.0	Alcoholic.
6135	..	2.3	2.2	2.1	0.11	4.0	0.4¼	0.7	0.2½	13.6	"
6138	..	2.9	2.7	2.1	0.11	4.1	0 4½	0.6½	0.3	15.9	"
6137	..	2.6	2 2	2.1	0 11	4.1	0.5	0.6½	0.3	13.3	"
6139	..	2.6	2.0	1.9	0.8	3.6	0.5	0.7	0.3	12.0	"
6140	..	2 5	2.0	2.0	0.11	4 0	0.3	0.7⅓	0.3	12.6	"
	..	2.5	2.0	2.0	0.9	2.6	0.5	0.6	0.3	13.0	"

LIST OF SPECIMENS.

Cat. No.	No. of Sp.	Locality.	Presented by	Nature of Spec'n.
3328	1	Matamoras, Mex.	Lt. Couch, U.S.A. (Berl. Coll.)	Alcoholic.
6135	1	"	" " "	"
6136	1	"	" " "	"
6137	1	"	" " "	"
6138	1	"	" " "	"
6139	1	"	" " "	"
6140	1	"	" " "	"

SCOTOPHILUS, LEACH.

Scotophilus, LEACH, Trans. Linn. Soc. Lond. XIII, 1822, 71. (Type *S. kuhlii.*)
Vesperus, KEYSERLING & BLASIUS, Wirbel-Thiere Europas, 1840, 49.
Vesperugo, KEYSERLING & BLASIUS, Wirbel-Thiere Europas, 1840, 45.

Molars less than $\frac{6}{6}$; head flat, broad; lips swollen; tragus bluntish; internal basal lobe of ear rounded, obtuse.

Fig. 23.

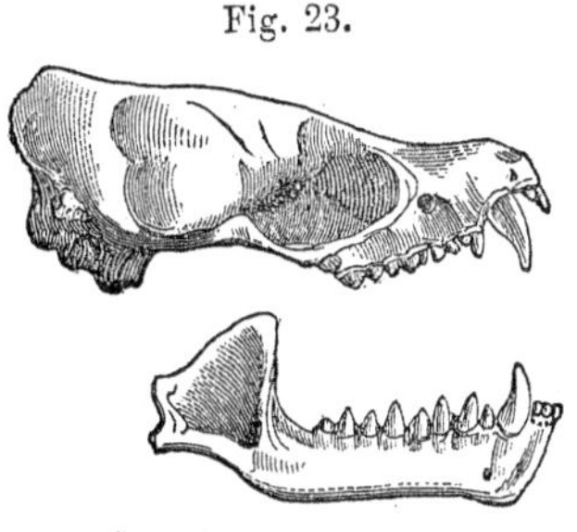

Scotophilus carolinensis.

The genus *Scotophilus* is closely allied to *Vespertilio* and differs chiefly from it in the heaviness of its wing membranes, and in the thick leathery ear and tragus, which possess a tendency to develop in width rather than in height. The distinction between these genera is really difficult to describe, though readily recognizable upon observation. The difference between their facial expression might be compared to that between a mastiff and terrier dog: the former is massive with broad head, pendulous lips and wide ears; the latter is more slender, with a narrower face and delicate and upright ears.

The type of the genus *Scotophilus* of Leach is his *S. kuhlii*, described without reference to any previous author, and without indication of habitat. It is impossible to say, therefore, whether he refers to the *Vespertilio kuhlii* of Natterer (1819), a European species, or whether he applied the name to a second and different species. As however the diagnosis appears not incongruous with the European *kuhlii*, and as this was probably known to him at the time, we may adopt the former supposition. This species falls in the genus *Vesperugo* of Keyserling & Blasius.

It is not a little remarkable that the paper of Leach, in which the genus *Scotophilus* is described, should have apparently escaped the attention of Continental authors; to such a degree, indeed, that they credit the genus to Gray as of 1842,[1] and consequently subsequent to *Vesperugo* of Keyserling & Blasius, instead of being long prior to it. I have found no reference in any of the standard European authors to the species *Scotophilus kuhlii* of Leach, except by Tomes, as in Pr. Zool. Soc., 1861, 35, etc.

The following is the arrangement of the species:—

a. (VESPERUS, Keys. & Blasius.) Central incisors larger than lateral; upper molars 4; base of foot with rounded swelling—

Ears sub-erect	. . . .	*S. carolinensis.*
Ears turned outwards	. . . . . .	*S. fuscus.*

b. (VESPERUGO, Keys. & Blasius.) Central incisors equal to the lateral; upper molars 5; base of foot without rounded swelling—

Central incisor bicuspid	Tragus slender, erect	*S. georgianus.*
	Tragus thick, obtuse	*S. noctivagans.*
Central incisor unicuspid	. . . .	*S. hesperus.*

Scotophilus carolinensis, GEOFF.

The Carolina Bat.

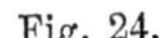

Fig. 24.

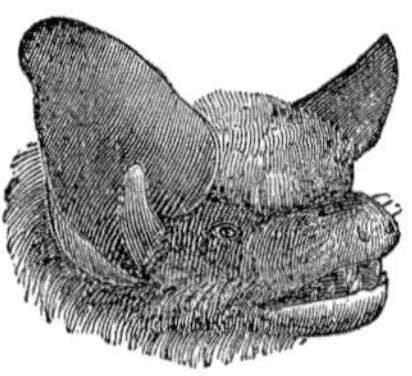

Fig. 25.

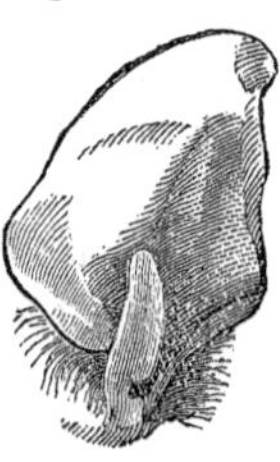

Vespertilio carolinensis, GEOFF. ST. HILAIRE, Ann. du Mus. VIII, 1806, 193, pl. xlvii, f. 7.—HARLAN, Fauna Amer. 1825, 9.—GODMAN, Amer. Nat. Hist. 1826, 67.—LECONTE, Cuv. An. King. (McMurtrie) I, 1831, 431. —HARLAN, Month. Amer. Jour. Geol. and Nat. Sc. I, 1831, 218.—IB., Med. and Phy. Research. 1831, 28.—COOPER, Ann. Lyceum N. H., N. Y.

[1] Ann. and Mag. N. H., X, 1842, 257.

IV, 1837, 60.—DeKay, Nat. Hist. N. Y. (Zool.), 1842, 10, pl. ii, f. 1.—Desm. Mam. 1820, 136.—Temminck, Monog. II, 1835, 237.—Leconte, Proc. Acad. Nat. Sci., 1855, 434.—Wagner, Schreb. Säug. V, 1855, 753.

Description.—Head flat; nostrils emarginated; ear not quite as long as the head, broad at base, obtusely rounded at tip; tragus straight on the inner side, slightly convex on the outer, nearly half the height of the auricle and notched at the outer lower part. The inferior anterior part does not reach the angle of the mouth. Nostrils rather large, separated by an emarginate space. Tip of tail exserted.

Hair uniformly bicolored, except on the ears and margins of the body; on the back it is dark plumbeous at base, the upper half varying from dusky cinereous to dark brown. On the head the hair is more lanuginous and thickly set; it covers half the posterior part of the ears, and runs on almost to the nose; in the latter portion it is longer, and bicolored, as in the back.

Fur on the under surface lighter than on the upper. A light brown tinge tips each hair—the lower two-thirds being dark cinereous, verging to black. As the hair in front approaches the head it also becomes woolly like that on the back, and has a tendency to assume one color. This appearance terminates at the anterior inferior border of the ear.

Interfemoral membrane ample; basal fifth furred posteriorly, faintly dotted with minute tufts of hair elsewhere. Terminal joint of tail exserted. Wing membrane attached to base of toes. In many specimens the calcaneum is well developed.

Fig. 26.

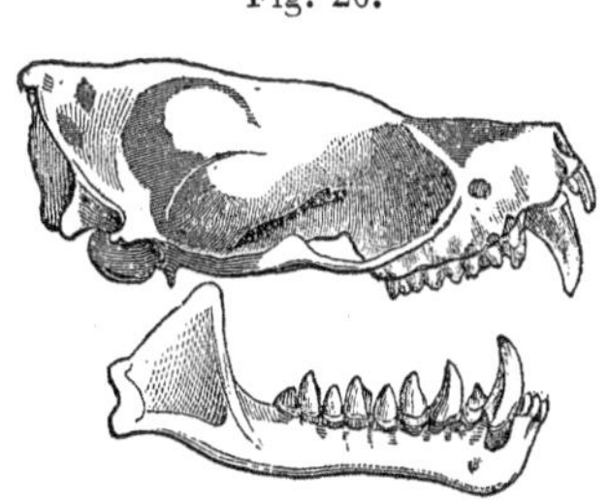

Scotophilus carolinensis. (Magnified.)

Skull.—The skull is large, and slightly crested behind.

Dentition.

Molars $\frac{4}{5}$. Canines $\frac{1}{1}$. Incisors $\frac{4}{6}$. Canines $\frac{1}{1}$. Molars $\frac{4}{5}$ = 32 teeth.

Upper Jaw.—The central incisors are large, converging, irregularly bifid—the internal cusp being the longer; the laterals not more than one-third the length of the centrals. Canines unicuspid, with minute basal cusps. First molar narrower than the other three, answering to the third premolar of *Vespertilio.*

Lower Jaw.—Incisors 6, trifid, crowded. Canines large, simple. Molars 5, the first two smaller and simple, increasing in size from the canines. Molars proper not peculiar.

I feel some hesitation in separating *S. carolinensis* from *S. fuscus.* They may yet prove to be the same, in which case *S. carolinensis* must be considered a synonym of *S. fuscus.*

MEASUREMENTS.

Current number.	Original number.	From tip of nose to tail.	Length of tail.	Length of forearm.	Length of tibia.	Length of longest finger.	Length of thumb.	Height of ear.	Height of tragus.	Expanse.	Nature of specimen.
1	..	2.2	1 8	1.8	0.7	3.0	0.4	0.6	0.2	12.0	Dry.
4214	..	2.6	1.6	1 9	0 7	3.0	0.4	0.6	0.3	10 0	"
4732	..	2.3	1.6	1.9	0 7	3 0	0.4	0.7	0.3	10.0	"
75	..	2 5	1.7	1.9	0.7	3 0	0.4	0.7	0.3	?	"
5135	..	2.4	1.6	1.8	0 7	3.0	0.4	0.6	0.3	?	"

LIST OF SPECIMENS.

Cat. No.	No. of Sp.	Locality.	Presented by	Nature of Specimen.
5521	1	Carlisle, Pa.	S. F. Baird.	Dry.
5135	1	Washington, D. C.	" "	"
4214	1	Neosho Falls.	B. F. Goss.	"
5543	5	Nebraska.	Dr. Cooper.	Alcoholic.
4732	1	"U. S."	Maj. Leconte.	Dry.
5542	1	?	C. Girard.	Alcoholic.

Scotophilus fuscus, PALISOT DE BEAUVOIS.

The Brown Bat.

Fig. 27.

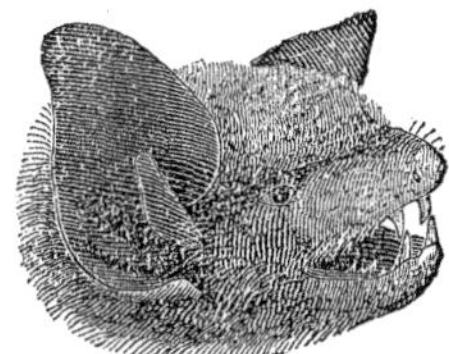

Fig. 28.

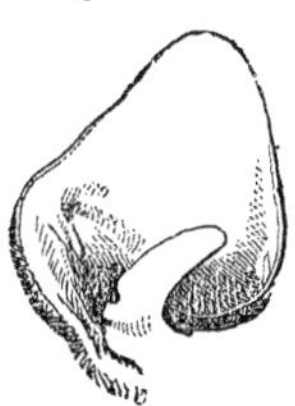

Vespertilio fuscus, PALISOT DE BEAUV. Cat. Peale's Mus. 1796, 14.—LECONTE, Proc. Acad. Nat. Sci. Phila. 1855, 437.

Vespertilio arcuatus, SAY, Long's Exp. R'ky Mts. 1823, 167.

Vespertilio phaiops, RAF. Amer. Month. Mag. 1818, 445 (not TEMM. Monog. Mam. II, 1835, 234).—LECONTE, Proc. Acad. Nat. Sci. Phila. 1855, 437.—WAGNER, Schreb. Säug. V, 1855, 756.

Vespertilio ursinus, TEMM. Monog. Mam. II, 1835, 234.—WAGNER, Schreb. Saüg. V, 1855, 756.—MAX PR. WIED, Archiv Naturg. 1861, 190.

Vespertilio gryphus, FR. CUV., Ann. du Mus. I, 1837, 15.—WAGNER, Schreb. Säug. V. 1855, 749.

Vespertilio caroli, LECONTE (not TEMM.), Proc. Acad. Nat. Sci. Phila. 1855, 437.

Scotophilus greeni (?) GRAY, Cat. Mam. British Museum, 1842.

Description.—Ears moderate, leathery, semi-erect, turned slightly outwards, convex on the inner border, nearly straight on the outer, in some slightly emarginate; the lower third of this portion is slightly revolute outwards; basal lobe well developed. Tragus nearly half as high as auricle, straight on inner border, moderately convex and diverging on outer; sometimes the tip is more acute than in other species, but is never pointed; in some specimens it has a very slight incurvation.

The coloring is very similar to *S. carolinensis*, being dark plumbeous at base, with chestnut-brown tips above, and light cinereous, fawn russet brownish tips below. This coloration exhibits some slight differences in different specimens: thus the back may be more of a light russet, and that in front more of a whitish hue. The extent of the plumbeous is also subject to variation, in some specimens occupying but the lower third of the hair; while in others—and this is more apt to occur on the front—

the tips only will be of a different color. The fur is soft and long, running up the back of the ears one-half their height in many specimens, in others not more than a third that distance. The basal part of the triangular interfemoral membrane behind is hairy, the rest naked. Calcaneum weak. No extension of the fur upon the wing membrane. Thumb and foot moderate. Back of foot very slightly haired.

These variations in the coloration of this species enable the observer to arrange the specimens into three groups according to the style of coloring of the fur. Thus the 1st group has chestnut-brown tips on the back, with grayish-white tips on the belly; 2d, olive-brown tips on back, with fawn russet tips on the belly, intermingled with whitish; and 3d, deep chestnut-brown both above and below, that of the front being but a shade lighter than that of the back. In the specimen, No. 5966, Williamstown, Mass., the tips of the fur is everywhere white at the tip.

Both *S. carolinensis* and *fuscus* resemble *S. serotinus* of Europe. The shape of the ear and tragus are very similar, and the character of the face and tumidity of lips the same in all. The latter species, however, is of a larger size than the others, and the fur is almost entirely unicolored—that is, there being little or no difference between the coloration of the base and the tip of each hair.

Dentition, similar to that of preceding species.

Major Leconte, in his "Observations on the Bats of North America," claims the specific name *fuscus*, for what was formerly known as the *V. arcuatus*, Say. In my attempt to include several supposed distinct forms under one head, I have chosen the same name.

Palisot de Beauvois, as early as 1796, describes a species—*V. fuscus*—in an old pamphlet catalogue, which, being but little known, had received no attention prior to Major Leconte's quotation. The description in this forgotten brochure does not correspond very well with that of *Scotophilus:* for the number of incisors in the upper jaw is less than the number actually present. But this objection has not the importance that at first sight it might appear to possess, inasmuch as the little incisor, situated close to the canine, very frequently escapes observation—it being almost completely hidden in the growth of the adjacent gum. This slight omission I think in nowise affects the diagnosis, any more than the fact that the neglect of naturalists for a long time to notice the minute premolar behind the canine of the upper jaw of *L. cinereus* and *noveboracensis* would affect the identity of those species.

Temminck's species, *V. ursinus* and the *V. phaiops* of Rafinesque, I consider to be the same as the one under consideration. It would appear strange that these two forms should be united, when the bicolored hair of the first, as described by Temminck, would at once separate it from the unicolored fur of the second.[1] Major Leconte has indeed separated them; but in the individuals labelled by him, now before me, I have not been successful in observing any such difference as those mentioned above. I have, therefore, taken *V. ursinus* to be a true synonym of *S. fuscus*, and the form mentioned by Temminck as the *V. phaiops*, Raf., to be a species that has not been observed in North America, and is probably a member of another fauna.

In the memoir above noticed, Major Leconte has made a laudable effort to identify the species, the result of the labors of European authors, and thus relieve this subject of its intricate synonomy. With this object in view, he has dwelt upon and developed points not mentioned by the original describers. Thus, in speaking of the shape of the outer border of the ear, he says:—

"The *fuscus* has the ear somewhat triangular, very concave on the outer edge, and emarginate near the tip.

"The *ursinus* ear oval, entire; that is to say not at all emarginate, the orillon acinaciform and obtuse.

"The *phaiops* ear somewhat triangular, sinuous or bi-emarginate on the outer edge, orillon oblong, blunt.

"The *caroli* has the ears ovate, emarginate behind almost from the tip to the base, and the orillon lanceolate, blunt, rounded at the point, a little curved on the posterior edge."

While acknowledging that these differences may exist, I do not consider them to be constant. In a species so extensively distributed—and in a family so well known for its Protean tendencies—as that to which *S. fuscus* belongs, slight and variable changes, confined entirely to the parts of the ear, are hardly sufficient data for these separations.

[1] *Vide* Appendix.

Had Major Leconte been an original laborer in this field, and the material now before me been at his disposal, I can scarcely believe that he would have described from it four new species of bats. He would rather have looked upon the minute differences above mentioned as of no specific value.

I may mention here that *V. caroli*, Temm., is not a species of *Scotophilus*—Major Leconte being in error respecting the dentition. The dentition, according to its describer, is

$$\text{Molars } \frac{6}{6}.\ \text{ Canines } \frac{1}{1}.\ \text{ Incisors } \frac{4}{6}.\ \text{ Canines } \frac{1}{1}.\ \text{ Molars } \frac{6}{6} = 38 \text{ teeth.}$$

It is very probably a true *Vespertilio.*

Fig. 29.

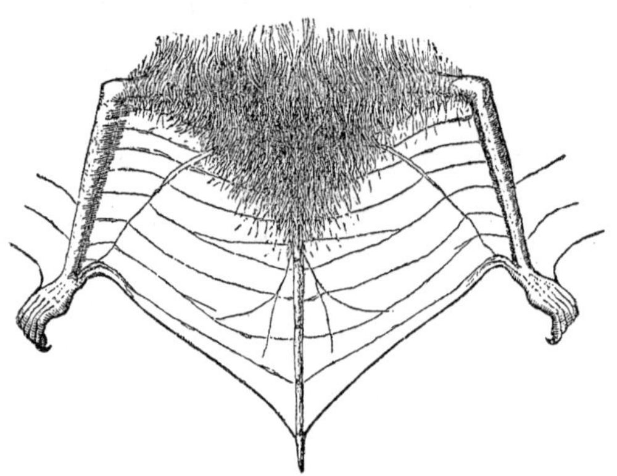

S. fuscus.

MEASUREMENTS.

Current number.	Original number.	From tip of nose to tail.	Length of tail.	Length of forearm.	Length of tibia.	Length of longest finger.	Length of thumb.	Height of ear.	Height of tragus.	Expanse.	Nature of specimen.
4731	..	2.6	1.4	1.9	0.9	2 9	0 3	0.5	0.2½	10 0	Dry.
4734	..	2.9	1.5	1.9	0.9	3 0	0 5	0 6	0.3	11.0	"
4737	..	2.5	1.5	1.8	0.8	3.0	0 4	0.5	0.2½	10.0	"
4739	..	2.9	1.4	1 8	0 9	3 0	0 4	0 7	0.3	10 ½	"
473	..	2.6	1 4	1.6	0 7	3.0	0.4	0.5	0.3	?	"
?	..	2.7	1.5	1.7	0.8	3.0	0.4	0.5	0 3	11.0	"
3137	..	2.2	1.6	1.9	0.7	3.0	0.4	0 5	0.3	9.6	"
537	..	2.4	1.4	1.6	0 7	2.6	0.3	0.5	0.2½	?	"
424	..	3.0	1.4	2.9	0.8	3.0	0.4	0.6	0.3	10	"

LIST OF SPECIMENS.

Cat. No.	No. of Sp.	Locality.	Presented by	Nature of Specimen.
6192	1	Lake Winnipeg.	R. Kennicott.	Alcoholic.
5306	2	Williamstown, Mass.	S. H. Scudder.	"
5302	1	Westport, N. Y.	S. F. Baird.	"
5304	1	Carlisle, Pa.	S. F. Baird.	"
5307	1	Washington, D. C.	Col. Weaver.	"
5384	1	Washington, D. C.	T. R. Peale.	"
5306	1	Cleveland, O.	Dr. Kirtland.	"
5399	1	Mississippi.	Col. Wailes.	"
5310	1	Roane Co., Tenn.	Prof. Mitchell.	"
5332	3	Grand Coteau, La.	St. Charles College.	"
5311	1	St. Louis, Mo.	Dr. Geo. Engelmann.	"
5324	1	Ft. Riley, Kansas.	Henry Brandt.	"
5328	7	Nebraska.	Dr. J. G. Cooper.	"
5315	1	Milk River, Neb.	Dr. Hayden.	"
5317	2	Ft. Pierre, Neb.	Dr. J. Evans.	"
5309	1	Fort Towson, Ark.	Dr. Edwards.	"
5308	1	Fort Smith, Ark.	Dr. Shumard.	"
3271	1	Mo. of Poteau River.	"	"
6191 var	1	Brazos River, Tex.	"	"
5320	1	Puget Sound, W. T.	?	"
5325	1	Carson Valley, Nev.	Capt. J. H. Simpson.	"
5326	1	San Francisco, Cal.	H. B. Mollhauson.	"
5314	1	Posa Creek, Cal.	Dr. Heermann.	"
4337	1	United States.	Major Leconte.	"
4731	1	" "	"	"
4739	1	" "	"	"
4734	1	" "	"	"
5330	1	" "	?	"
5344–5	2	" [Cruz, Mex.	?	"
5411	1	El Mirador, near Vera	Dr. C. Sartorius.	"

Scotophilus georgianus, ALLEN.

The Georgian Bat.

Fig. 30.

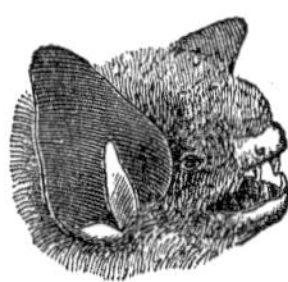

Fig. 31.

Vespertilio georgianus, FR. CUV. Ann. du Mus. 1832, 16.—LECONTE, Proc. Acad. Nat. Sci. Phila. 1855, 436.—WAGNER, Schreb. Säug. V, 1855, 750.

Vespertilio monticola, BACHMAN, Proc. Acad. Nat. Sci. 1841, 92.

Vespertilio crassus (?), FR. CUV. Ann. du Mus. 1832, 17.

Vespertilio salarii (?), FR. CUV. Ann. du Mus. 1832, 17.

Description.—Head flat, but not so heavy and thick as in other species of *Scotophilus*, moderately hairy; sides of face swollen, and studded with hair. Nose flat, broad, naked; nostrils small, oblique, opening sublaterally. Sides of mouth very slightly whiskered. Ears nearly naked, subelliptical, slightly convex on the inner, nearly straight on the outer border, which terminates near the mouth in a wart. Parts about the head light brown. Tragus straight, blunt, moderately divergent on its outer side. Thumb and feet large.

Fur thick, long and soft. Color dark rufous brown on back, brighter rufous in front; base of fur before and behind dark plumbeous. The fur extends to upper third of posterior surface of interfemoral membrane: the anterior surface of which is decorated with numerous small tufts arranged transversely. The fur of body also extends a slight distance upon the anterior surface of the wing membrane. Wings reach to base of toes; point of tail slightly exserted. Calcaneum moderate—its termination forms no lobe with the interfemoral membrane.

No. 7002 (included in 5297), a young specimen, Carlisle, Pa., is a variety with dark, faintly bicolored fur, of a grizzled olive-brown color.

Fig. 32.

S. georgianus.

Skull small, papery; flat, but less so than in other species of *Scotophilus*. There is a slight tendency to the shape of face peculiar to *Vespertilio*.

Dentition.

Molars $\frac{5}{5}$. Canines $\frac{1}{1}$. Incisors $\frac{4}{6}$. Canines $\frac{1}{1}$. Molars $\frac{5}{5}$ = 34 teeth.

Upper Jaw.—The incisors placed as usual, and of the same size. The centrals of equal size and so obscurely bifid that the lateral point seems more like a basal cusp. The lateral teeth cuspid and converging (there are some examples of the bicuspid lateral). Canines rather small, simple. First molar minute, unicuspid, but readily visible from the outside. The second premolar resembles the corresponding tooth in the other species; the remaining molars are not peculiar.

Lower Jaw.—Incisors trifid, not crowded. Canines small, with a basal cusp on either side. The premolars are rather small, and have minute points at their base, making them appear as though indistinctly tricuspid. Other molars as usual.

This species has been but imperfectly described by the authors above cited. Fr. Cuvier's diagnosis is quite incomplete, and would be undistinguishable from that of the smaller form of *V. subulatus*, had it not been that, from having sent the author the specimens from which the description was taken, Major Leconte was familiar with the type and afterwards gave a more exact description of the animal in the work above cited. He however was himself in error in some particulars, especially in making the dentition similar to that of *V. subulatus*, and in asserting that the last false molar of the upper jaw was bi-emarginated. I have before me a large series of specimens, some of which have Major Leconte's name attached, but in none of them have I found any internal basal bi-emarginate cusp as described by him.

Dr. Bachman's description of *V. monticola* applies well to *S. georgianus*, excepting in the measurements, which, in the case of the ear and tragus, are entirely too small in proportion to the size of the body. I have an alcoholic specimen, marked *V. monticola*, in the same handwriting as some other specimens purported to have been labelled by Dr. Bachman, which is beyond doubt *S. georgianus*—the ear and tragus being of the usual size.

MEASUREMENTS.

Current number.	Original number.	From tip of nose to tail.	Length of tail.	Length of forearm.	Length of tibia.	Length of longest finger.	Length of thumb.	Height of ear.	Height of tragus.	Expanse.	Nature of specimen.
5298	..	1.8	1.6	1.4	0.6	2.4	0 4	0.5	0.3	9.0	Alcoholic.
5297	..	1.6	1.6	1.4	0.6	2.4	0.4	0.5	0.3	8.9	"
5981	..	1.6	1.6	1.4	0.6	2 3	0.4	0.7	0 3½	8.6	"
5982	..	1.6	1.5	1.4	0.6	2.3	0.4	0.6	0.3	8.6	"
5983	..	1.6	1.5	1.4	0 7	2:2	0.4	0.5	0.3	8.6	"
5318	..	1.6	1.6	1.4	0.7	2.3	0.4	0.5	0.3	9.0	"
5339	..	1.8	1.6	1.3	0 6	2.3	0.4	0.4½	0.3	9.3	"
5340	..	1.6	1.5	1.4	0.6	2.2	0.3	0.5	0.3	9 3	"
	..	1.6	1.6	1.3	0.6	2.2	0.3½	0.5	0.3	8.11	"
5341	..	1.6	1.6	1.3	0.7	2.2	0.4½	0.5	0.3	8.10	"

LIST OF SPECIMENS.

Cat. No.	No. of Sp.	Locality.	Presented by	Nature of Spec'n.
5297	36	Carlisle, Pa.	S. F. Baird.	In alcohol.
5433	1	"	" "	Dry skin.
5375	1	Washington.	?	In alcohol.
5298	1	"	C. Girard.	"
5440	1	Hampshire Co., Va.	M. M'Donald.	Dry skin.
5340	2	Clark Co., Va.	Dr. Kennerly.	In alcohol.
5339	1	Mount Vernon.	?	"
5341	1	Whitfield Co., Ga.	A. Gerhardt.	"
5442	1	Georgia.	W. Cooper.	Dry skin.
5343	1	New Orleans.	N. O. Acad.	In alcohol.
5401	1	St. Louis, Mo.	Dr. G. Engelmann.	"
5318	1	Cairo, Ill.	R. Kennicott.	"
5360	1	Poteau Creek, Ark.	Dr. G. C. Shumard.	"
5371	3	Matamoras, Mex.	Lt. Couch. (Berl. Col.)	"
5439	1	United States.	Major Leconte.	"

Fig. 33.

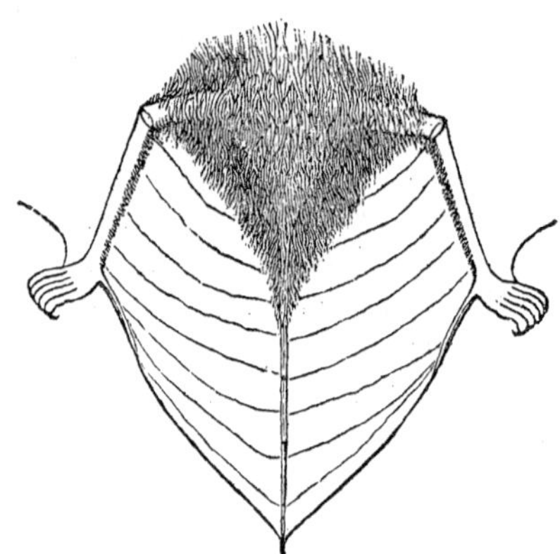

S. georgianus.

Scotophilus noctivagans, LECONTE.

The Silvery-haired Bat.

Fig. 34.

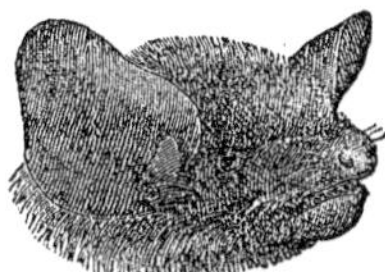

Fig. 35.

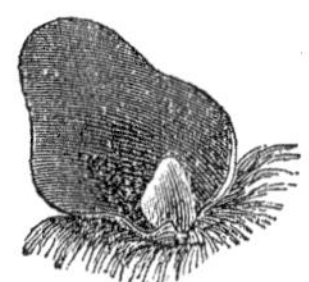

Vespertilio noctivagans, LECONTE, Cuv. An. Kingdom (McMurtrie ed.), I, June, 1831, 31.—COOPER, Ann. Lyc. N. Y. IV, 1837, 59.—DEKAY, Nat. Hist. N. Y. (Zool.), 1842, 9, pl. i, f. 1.—WAGNER, Schreb. Säug. V, 1855, 754.

Vespertilio auduboni, HARLAN, Month. Amer. Jour. Geol. Nat. Hist. I, Nov. 1831, 220, pl. ii.—IB. Med. and Physical Researches, 1835, 30, pl. iv.

Vespertilio pulverulentus, TEMM. Monog. Mam. II, 1835, 235.—LECONTE, Proc. Acad. Nat. Sci. 1855, 436.—PR. WIED, Archiv Naturg. 1861, 192.

Description.—Head flat, broad, and moderately haired. Snout naked; nostrils wide apart, and opening sublaterally; space between emarginate. The sides of the face slightly swollen. The auricle is an irregular oval. The inner border ascends upwards and *inwards* to a level with the top of the head, and then turns upwards and *outwards*, ending in an obtuse point. The outer border is smooth, and terminates inferiorly and internally in a thin ridge near the angle of the mouth. The lower half of this border folds irregularly upon itself, and bends so markedly inwards as to touch the tragus. The tragus is straight internally, strongly and abruptly convex externally—at its base narrow. It is but one-third the height of auricle, and nearly as broad as high. Skin of face and ears blackish, with the exception of the internal basal lobe of the latter, which is whitish.

Fur long and silky, with a marked tendency to become black, and in many specimens the extreme tip of each hair is the only part possessing a different hue—it being a pale gray or white. The fur is thicker on the back than in front, but the coloration is very similar on both sides: if there is any difference, it is where the shaft of the hair in front assumes in some individuals a plumbeous brown hue instead of the blackish. The characteristic pulverulent dash to the fur presents a striking appearance, and has given to this animal the popular appellation of the Silvery-haired Bat. The posterior part of the interfemoral membrane is thinly covered with short dark colored hairs: the anterior surface has upon it numerous minute tufts arranged linearly. Thumb small, slightly furred; foot moderate and furred on posterior surface.

Fig. 36.

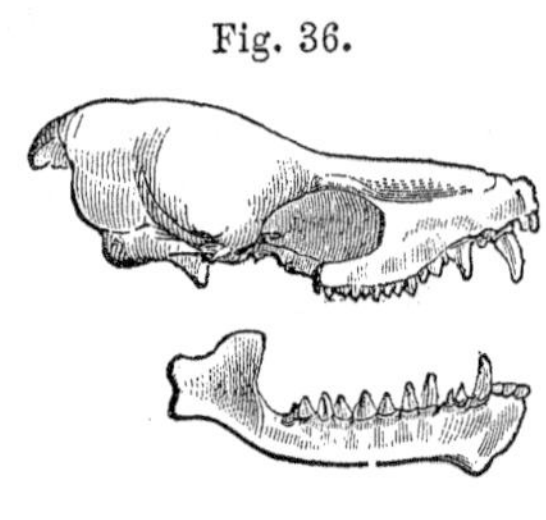

S. noctivagans.

Skull flat, not crested; two shallow depressions anteriorly.

Dentition.

Molars $\frac{5}{6}$. Canines $\frac{1}{1}$. Incisors $\frac{4}{6}$. Canines $\frac{1}{1}$. Molars $\frac{5}{6}$ = 36 teeth.

Upper Jaw.—Incisors two on either side of the median space, closely approximate to but not touching canines; nearly of the same length; centrals bifid, the teeth somewhat twisted on their axis so that the two cusps have something of an antero-posterior arrangement; the internal cusp is slightly longer than the external. The laterals are unicuspid, and have a basal cusp. The canines are simple and moderate. Of the five molars the first is very small, unicuspid, and crowded in between the canine and second premolar—it is visible from the outside. The second premolar has an external and internal cusp—the external longer than any external point of the molars proper, while the internal is shorter than any internal prominence. The other teeth as usual.

Lower Jaw.—Incisors not crowded, trifid. Canines moderate, with an anterior basal point. Of the three premolars the first is not so small as the second, which is about the size of the first premolar of the upper jaw; the third is about the height of the molars proper, and is simple. The other teeth as usual.

This species was described by Major Leconte and Dr. Harlan in the same year; but the description by the latter gentleman appeared five months subsequent to the former. *Vide* Cooper, *loc. cit.* Temminck's account followed the original description five years; he obtained his specimens from the Prince Max. Wied. I cannot learn upon what ground Major Leconte, in his "Observations," employed Temminck's specific name and discarded his own. It no doubt had, so far as I can judge from given data, the undisputed priority.

S. noctivagans bears some resemblance to *S. discolor*, Kuhl, a European species. The shapes of ear and tragus, the color of membranes, the powdered fur, and the haired interfemoral membrane are common to both; but in *S. noctivagans* the color of the hair is blackish instead of brown, and the dentition is different in many particulars.

No. 5359 is smaller than the other specimens, and has a more subulate tragus. The specimen was imperfect.

Habitat.—From the Atlantic coast to Rocky Mountains.

Varies very little in color and size. I have never seen any specimens "entirely black," a peculiarity of coloring stated by Major Leconte to sometimes occur.

MEASUREMENTS.

Current number.	Original number.	From tip of nose to tail.	Length of tail.	Length of forearm.	Length of tibia.	Length of longest finger.	Length of thumb.	Height of ear.	Height of tragus.	Expanse.	Nature of specimen.
3328	..	2.6	1.6	1.7	0.6	2.9	0.3	0.6	0 2	12.0	Dry.
4729	..	2.9	1.5	1.6	0.6	2.9	0.3	0.6	0.2½	12.0	"
746	..	2.5		1.7	0 6	2 9	0.3	0.6	0.2½		"
74	..	2.3	1.5	1.6	0.6	2.9	0.3	0.6½	0.3		"
2231	..										"
	..	2.0			0.6		0.3	0.6	0.3		"
1785	..	2.2	1.2	1.6	0.7	2.7	0.4	0.5½	0.2½		"

LIST OF SPECIMENS.

Cat. No.	No. of Sp.	Locality.	Presented by	Nature of Specimen.
5331	1	James Bay, H. B.	C. Drexler.	Alcoholic.
5295	2	Moose Factory, "	" "	"
5301	1	Middleboro', Mass.	J. W. P. Jenks.	"
5427	1	Carlisle, Pa.	S. F. Baird.	Dry.
5305	1	" "	David Miller.	Alcoholic.
5357	1	West Philadelphia.	W. S. Wood.	"
5290	1	Mt. Holly, N. J.	Dr. Geo. C. Brown.	"
5296	1	Washington, D. C.	W. Wilson.	"
3328	1	Illinois River.	R. Kennicott.	"
5291	1	St. Louis. Mo.	Dr. Engelmann.	"
5293	2	Nebraska.	Dr. J. G. Cooper.	"
5294	1	Platte River.	W. S. Wood.	"
5431	2	Fort Union, Neb.	Dr. F. V. Hayden.	"
5359	1	" "	" "	"
5316	2	" "	" "	"
5429	1	Yellowstone River.	Col. Vaughan.	"
5289	1	Puget Sound.	Dr. Kennedy.	"
5321	1	Fort Reading, Cal.	Dr. T. F. Hammond.	"
5292	1	United States.	?	"
4729	1	" "	Major Leconte.	"

Fig. 37.

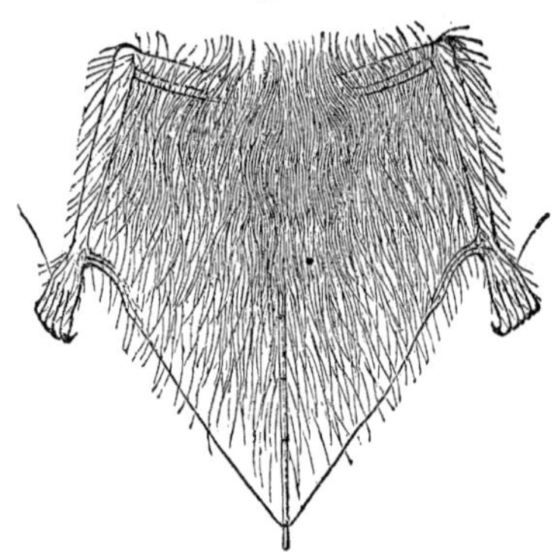

S. noctivagans.

Scotophilus hesperus, Allen.

The Western Bat.

Fig. 38.  Fig. 39.

Description.—Diminutive. Head small, flat; face blunt and stout, not hairy. Tragus short, blunt, slightly concave on inner, convex on outer border, causing it to incurve. Thumb small; nail dull and minute; foot very small; wing membranes attached to base of toes. Interfemoral membrane ample. A small excalcaneal lobe of membrane—the termination of calcaneum blending with the membrane. The tip of the tail is not exserted. Body rather slender.

The fur is somewhat scanty; it is thickest on the back where it is of an obscure dirty gray, blending in some individuals to a brownish color—that in front being thinner and of a lighter hue. The main bulk of the fur is of a dark plumbeous, the above-mentioned colors constituting the tips only.

Dentition.

Molars $\frac{5}{5}$. Canines $\frac{1}{1}$. Incisors $\frac{4}{6}$. Canines $\frac{1}{1}$. Molars $\frac{5}{5} = 34$ teeth.

Upper Jaw.—The incisors—both central and lateral—unicuspid, and of equal length; the canines moderately developed; the first premolar is very small, wedged in between the canine and the second premolar, which is large, as in other species of *Scotophilus;* the molars as usual.

Lower Jaw.—The incisors and canines not peculiar; the premolars two in number: the first is small, and is unicuspid, the second larger with an obscure basal cusp. The skull is eminently *Scotophiloid,* being flat and broad.

This bat resembles the *S. pipistrellus,* of Europe, in the contour of the head, the shape of the ear and tragus, the smallness and shape of the thumb and nail, the character of the interfemoral membrane, and in the style of coloring. The greater part of the fur in both is of dark plumbeous, the tip alone being a hue at variance with it. These tips in *S. hesperus* are brownish-gray and fawn, in *S. pipistrellus* being a rich olive-brown. In size it corresponds to that small European group with incurved tragus and rounded ear, of which *S. alcythoe* and *S. aristippe* are members. It differs from it, however, in the additional molar on the upper jaw. *S. hesperus*, therefore, is a form uniting, so far as can now be determined, the peculiarities of *S. pipistrellus* and *S. alcythoe* and *aristippe.*

MEASUREMENTS.

Current number.	Original number.	From tip of nose to tail.	Length of tail.	Length of forearm.	Length of tibia.	Length of longest finger.	Length of thumb.	Height of ear.	Height of tragus.	Expanse.	Nature of specimen.
5406	..	1.4	1.0	1.1	0.5	1.8	0.1	0.3	0.1½	7.0	
6015	..	1.4	?	1.1	0.5	1.6	0.1½	0.5½	0.1½	?	
5510	..	1.9	0.11	1.4	0.4	2.0	0.1½	0.4	0.1	7.0	

LIST OF SPECIMENS.

Cat. No.	No. of Sp.	Locality.	Presented by	Nature of Spec'n.
5406	1	Ft. Yuma, Cal.	Maj. G. H. Thomas.	Alcoholic.
5510	1	Posa Creek, Cal.	Dr. A. L. Heermann.	Dry.
5509	1	" " "	" "	"

Fig. 40.

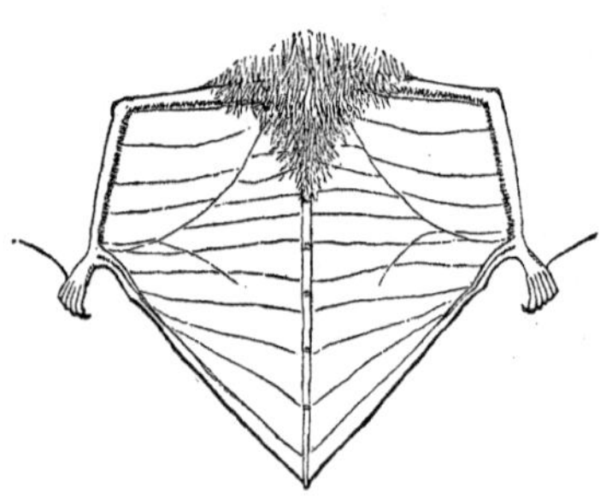

S. hesperus.

A bat, labelled 5345, Cass Co., Mo., presented by Dr. P. R. Hoy, presents peculiarities so marked that it cannot be assigned to any of the foregoing species. It belongs, however, to the group characterized by the small and equal superior incisors, of which *S. georgianus* and *S. hesperus* are the representatives. Indeed, the dentition throughout is similar to that seen in *S. georgianus;* and the *tout ensemble* of the animal indicates that it has a closer affinity to the former than to the latter of these species.

The head is flat and broad; lips slightly tumid; nostrils opening sublaterally, placed near the lip; the snout rather thick, and scarcely if at all emarginated; auricles of a light brown color, not quite as long as head, subulate, tip turned slightly outwards; internal basal border *not bluntish and rounded as in other species of Scotophilus, but markedly and sharply produced, as in Vespertilio.* Tragus similar to that of *S. georgianus*, short, stout; outer border strongly convex. Wing membrane of a blackish-brown color, attached to base of toes; foot rather large. Interfemoral membrane ample. Termination of calcaneum not abrupt. Tip of tail exserted, half the length of terminal caudal segment. Color very similar to that of *V. subulatus*—the fur of the back being more olive.

The above brief description agrees with that of *S. georgianus*, on the one hand, in the dentition, shape of tragus and style of wing membrane; with that of *V. subulatus*, on the other, in the shape of auricle, and in the coloring of the fur.

I have deemed it sufficient to thus indicate the peculiarities of this individual, without venturing upon a specific name, preferring to await the receipt of additional specimens.

VESPERTILIO, KEYSERLING & BLASIUS.

Vespertilio, KEYSERLING & BLASIUS, Wirbel thiere Europas, 1840, 17.

Molars $\frac{6}{6}$; skull inflated, raised above the line of the nasal bones; internal basal lobe of ear sharply defined, more or less acute.

Fig. 41.

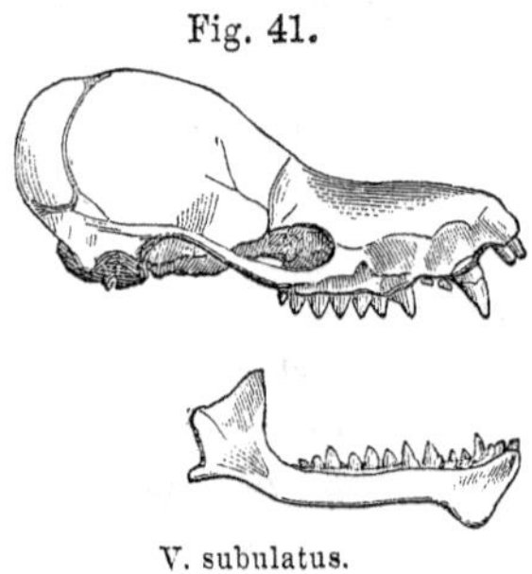

V. subulatus.

The term *Vespertilio* has been variously applied by authors. As employed by Linnæus, it represented a group now considered to be an entire order—*Cheiroptera.* When Geof. St. Hilaire revised the bats, he restricted the name to the naked-nosed forms with the tail inclosed within the interfemoral membrane. It has again been divided by numerous authors, among whom may be mentioned Isidore Geoffroy, Temminck, Gray, Keyserling & Blasius, until at present as properly restricted by the latter accomplished naturalists, it is used to designate a small but well defined group, the members of which embrace the most delicate forms of *Vespertilionidæ.* Owing to the fact that species of the genus have a widely spread distribution, minute differences in form and color in specimens brought from distant localities have been made of more importance than they deserve. Species have thus sprung up, many of which have never been identified, and serve only to retard progression by a useless synonymy.

Some of the many so-called species of this country I have been enabled to determine; with others, however, I have not been so successful. The names of the former are mentioned as synonyms to those having the priority. With the remainder I am obliged to content myself with merely naming, viz.: *V. subflavus*, *V.*

crassus, Fr. Cuv.; *V ferrugineus*, *V. erythrodactylus*, Temm.;[1] *V. megalotis*, *V. phaiops*, *V. melanotis*, *V. cyanopterus*, *V. mystax*, Raf.;[1] *V. virginianus*, *V. leibii*, Bachman.[1]

We cannot do better here than introduce the remarks of Major Leconte, inserted at the close of his Observations quoted above, relative to these species:—

"Of bats described by others, the following with but one exception, I have never seen. Dr. Bachman, in the eighth vol. Jour., mentions four species. *V. monticola*, he says, resembles Say's bat; what species he calls by that name I cannot discover. *V. virginianus* seems to be the *V. humeralis* of Rafinesque. I have not seen this last for several years, and therefore cannot pronounce definitely concerning it. The *V. leibii* and *V. californicus* are equally unknown. Of M. Rafinesque's species, it is impossible to determine the following; there is good reason to doubt, however, whether they are distinct from others which are well known: *V. cyanopterus*, *V. melanotis*, *V. calcaratus*, *V. phaiops* (afterwards described in his Annals of Nature, No. 1, as his *Eptisecus melanops*); *V. megalotis*, *V. mystax* (afterwards called, in the Journal de Physique, Vol. LXXXVIII, p. 417, *Hyperodon mystax* and *Eptisecus melas*). M. Cuvier's *V. salarii* may be the *fuscus*, and his *subflavus* the *carolinensis;* his *crassus* likewise I cannot determine. M. Temminck's *V. erythrodactylus*, Temm. Vol. II, p. 235, remains amongst those unknown to me."

Such are the conclusions of an accomplished naturalist! After careful study he can only conjecture what *might* have been the meaning of his authors. Rafinesque, with whom rests the greater part of the blame of this faulty and careless observation, seems to have been utterly regardless of the existence of specific characters. Many of his descriptions are mere words, seldom conveying any definite impression to the mind; and if they are so far successful, it is rarely a correct one. But the work of this eccentric naturalist was excusable when compared with that of F. Cuvier. This gentleman had received from Major Leconte a collection of North American Bats, the new species of which he described.[2] But so carelessly was this work performed that out of his descriptions, six in number, the donor could recognize but two—*V. georgianus* and *V. gryphus*, the latter being a synonym of *S. fuscus*. The

[1] *Vide* Appendix (for all these descriptions). [2] *Vide* Appendix.

descriptions of Dr. Bachman are also very imperfect. The most valuable points—such as the attachment of wing membrane to the feet, and the number of molars—being omitted.

In the new species which I have deemed it necessary to introduce, I much regret that from the above list I could not retain any names. As objectionable as it is to increase the number of species of *Vespertilionidæ* when there are so many yet undetermined, it would be still more so to apply to forms thought to be distinct names to which no specific characters have been attached, or which, if applying to good species, are descriptive of peculiarities not found in those about to be given.

The species may be arranged as follows:—

1. Internal basal lobe of ear acute.	
a. Point of tail very slightly exserted. Ears longer than head . .	*V. evotis.*
a. Point of tail very slightly exserted. Ears as long as head . .	*V. nitidus.*
b. Point of tail decidedly exserted.	
Tragus linear, turned outward	*V. subulatus.*
Tragus linear, erect.	
Color beneath chestnut-brown	*V. yumanensis.*
Color beneath whitish	*V. affinis.*
2. Internal basal lobe of ear obtuse, rounded	*V. lucifugus.*

Vespertilio evotis, Allen, n. s.

Fig. 42.

Fig. 43.

Description.—Head rather small; face pointed, moderately whiskered; snout produced; ears large, high, erect, oval, not turning outwardly; long, sub-acuminate slightly diverging tragus; thumb slender; foot of moderate size; ample interfemoral membrane; last joint of tail exserted. The membranes are of a light brown color, tending in some to a darker hue. Hair long and soft, plumbeous at base behind, with light brown tips inclined to yellowish toward the head.

The fur in front is dark maroon, or black at base with whitish tips. The basal third of the ear is covered with hair at base: at the base of the interfemoral membrane behind a tuft of hair is seen.

In two specimens the fur had a darker tinge, the tips behind being dark olive-brown, the base being black.

This species has the largest ear of any of the American species of *Vespertilio.*

The cranium is greatly inflated; the face slender and pointed.

Dentition.

Molars $\frac{6}{6}$. Canines $\frac{1}{1}$. Incisors $\frac{4}{6}$. Canines $\frac{1}{1}$. Molars $\frac{6}{6} = 38$ teeth.

Upper Jaw.—The incisors are grouped in pairs near the canines, separated by an open space. The centrals are markedly bifid, the laterals obscurely so. Of the premolars the first two are very small, the second being the smaller; the third is larger, compressed and bicuspid, the outer cusp much the larger, and longer than any point of the molars proper. The remaining molars not peculiar.

Lower Jaw.—Incisors trifid, the one adjacent to the canine on either side obscurely quadrilobed. Canines with a small basal cusp behind. The premolars small, the two anterior most so, the third is slender; basal ridge thick.

No specimens have been received from localities east of the Rocky Mountains. It appears to be comparatively common along the Pacific coast from Puget Sound to Lower California.

MEASUREMENTS.

Current number.	Original number.	From tip of nose to tail.	Length of tail.	Length of forearm.	Length of tibia.	Length of longest finger.	Length of thumb.	Height of ear.	Height of tragus.	Expanse.	Nature of specimen.
5390*a*	..	1.8	1.5½	1.5	0.8	2.3	0.4	0 8	0.5	9.0	Alcoholic.
5390*b*	..	1.6	1.4	1.5	0.8	2 3	0.3½	0.6	0.5	9.0	"
5390*c*	..	1.6	1.4	1.5	0.8	2.3	0.3½	0.8	0.4½	9.0	"
5389	..	1.6	1.6	1.6	0.7	2.3	0.3	0.11	0.5½	9.6	"
5392*a*	..	1.6	1.6	1.6	0.7½	2.4	0.3	0.8½	0.6	10.0	"
5392*b*	..	1.6	1.6	1.6	0 7	2.3	0.3	0.9	0.6	10.0	"
5392*c*	..	1.6	1.6	1.5	0.6	2 3	0.3	0.8	0.6	10.0	"
5391*a*	..	1.6	1.6	1.5	0.6	2.3	0.3	0.9	0 6	8.7	"
5391*b*	..	1.6	1.6	1.5	0.6	2.3	0.2½	0.9	0.6	8.6	"
5413	..	1.4	1.4	1.5	0 7	2 1	0.2½	0.9	0.5	?	"
	..	1.6	1.6	1.5	0.7	2.3	0.3	0.11	0.5	8.9	"
5395	..	1.6	1.6	1.5	0.8	2.3	0.3	0.11	0.5	9.0	"
5413	..	?	2.0	1.6	?	2.6	0.5	0.7½	0 4	8 6	Dry.
1789	..	2.0	1.3	1.6	0.8	2 0	0.5	0.7	0.3	?	"

LIST OF SPECIMENS.

Cat. No.	No. of Sp.	Locality.	Presented by	Nature of Spec'm.
5392	3	Upper Missouri.	Dr. Hayden.	Alcoholic.
5390	3	Puget Sound. [B. Surv.)		"
5391	2	East of Colville. (N. W.	Dr. C. B. Kennerly.	"
5389	1	Monterey, Cal.	A. S. Taylor.	"
5387	2	Cape St. Lucas.	John Xantus.	"
5395	1	?	?	"
5413	1	Mts. of N. Mexico.	Capt. Pope.	Dry.

Fig. 44.

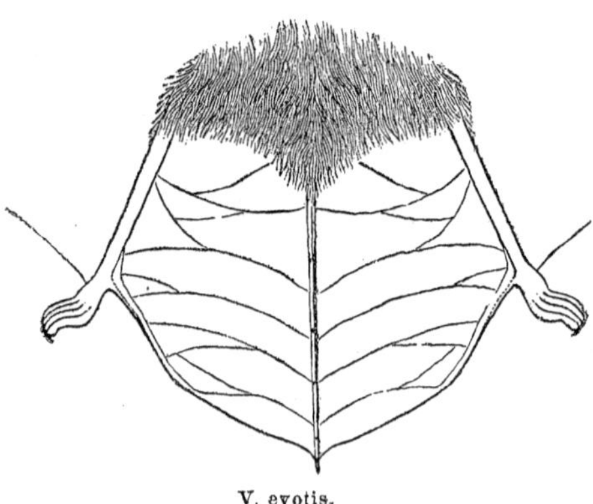

V. evotis.

Vespertilio subulatus, SAY.

The Little Brown Bat.

Fig. 45. Fig. 46.

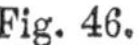

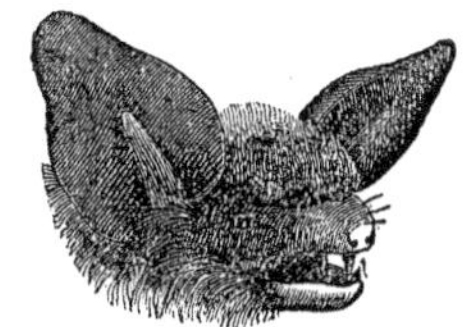

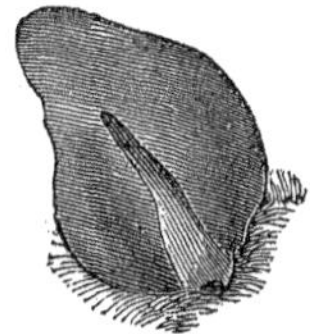

Vespertilio subulatus, SAY, Long's Exp. to Rk'y Mts. II, 1823, 65 (note).—HARLAN, Fauna Americana, 1825, 22.—RICHARDSON, Fauna Bor. Amer. I, 1829, 3.—GODMAN, Amer. Nat. Hist. I, 1831, 71.—COOPER, Ann. Lyc. N. Y. IV, 1837, 61.—DEKAY, Nat. Hist. N. Y. (Zool.) 1842, 8.—WAGNER, Schreb. V, 1855, 750.—LECONTE, Proc. Acad. Nat. Sci. Phila. 1855, 436.

Vespertilio californicus, BACHMAN, Journ. Phila. Acad. Nat. Sci. 1842, 280.—PEALE, U. S. Explor. Exp. (Mam.) 1858, 3.

Vespertilio caroli, TEMM. Monog. II, 1835, 237.—WAGNER, Schreb. Saüg. V, 1855, 749.

Vespertilio domesticus, GREEN, Cab. Nat. Hist. II, 290.

Description.—Head light, moderate size; face whiskered; ear smaller than in *V. evotis,* turned slightly outwards; tragus erect, half the height of the ear; the interfemoral membrane smallest, the point of tail exserted.

The fur is not so thick as in *V. evotis.* The base of the hair behind is of a dark plumbeous color, tips olive-brown; the base in front is of the same hue, blending into a whitish-yellow tip. The color is subject to little variation; the olive-brown of the back is, in some specimens, of a lighter hue. The distribution as in other species.

Dentition as in *V. evotis.*

The specimens of *V. subulatus* arrange themselves into two groups, one of which may be considered typical, the other tending in the shape of ear to the *preceding* species. Indeed the change from one species to the other is so gradual that it is difficult to assign the boundary to each. I have included under *V. subulatus* a number of specimens which have the ear higher than those from which the description has been taken, but agreeing with *V. subulatus* in other particulars.

Hab.—Very common, especially in the country east of the Rocky Mountains, where it is the most abundant of the species of *Vespertilio*.

MEASUREMENTS.

Current number.	Original number.	From tip of nose to tail.	Length of tail.	Length of forearm.	Length of tibia.	Length of longest finger.	Length of thumb.	Height of ear.	Height of tragus.	Expanse.	Nature of specimen.
5382	..	1.6	1.4	1.4	0.7½	2.1	0.3	0.7	0.6	9.0	
5384	..	1.6	1.4	1.4	0.7½	2.3	0.3	0.7	0.3	9.0	
5346	..	1.6	1.4	1.4	0.7½	2.2	0.3	0.7	0.3	9 0	
	..	1.8	1.4½	1.4	0.7	2.3	0.3	0.6½	0.3	9.0	
5385	..	1.6	1.5	1.3	0 4½	2.1	0.2½	0.7	0.3	8.0	
5370	..	1.6	1.4	1.2½	0.4½	2 2	0.3	0 7½	0.3	9.0	
5393	..	1.6	1.5	1.4½	0 5	2.3	0.3	0.7	0.3	9.0	
5352	..	1.10	1.8	1.6	0.5½	2.4	0.3	0.7	0.4	9.2	

Fig. 47.

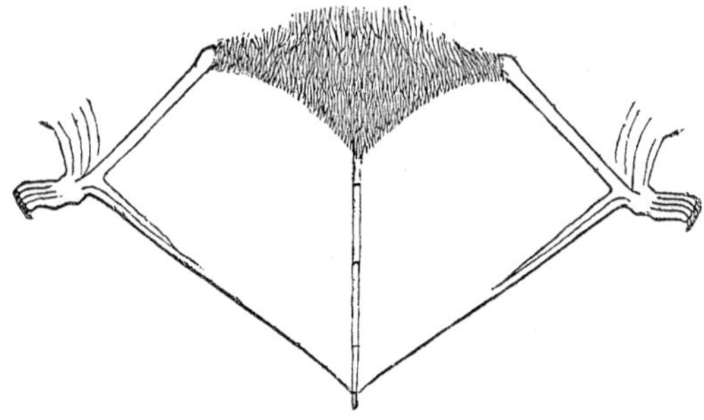

V. subulatus.

LIST OF SPECIMENS.

Cat. No.	No. of Sp.	Locality.	Presented by	Nature of Specimen.
5384	1	Nova Scotia.	Dr. Gilpin.	Alcoholic.
5370	1	Brunswick, Me.	A. S. Packard.	"
5385	1	Elizabethtown, N. Y.	S. F. Baird.	"
6322	1	Nebraska.	Dr. Cooper.	"
5385	1	Phillipsburg, Pa.	A. Brakeley.	"
5382	1	Bradford, Pa.	C. C. Martin.	"
5381	1	Meadville, Pa.	J. F. Thickstun.	"
7196	1	Beaufort, S. C.	Dr. Hayden?	Dry.
7197	1	" "	" "	"
3721	1	Michipico, L. Sup.	C. A. Hubbard.	"
5355	1	Portage, Lake Sup.	B. A. Hoopes.	Alcoholic.
5351	1	Upper Mis. River, Ill.	R. Kennicott.	"
5312	1	Racine, Wis.	Dr. P. R. Hoy.	"
5500	1	Gross Isl., Mich.	C. Fox.	Dry.
5318	1	" "	" "	Alcoholic.
5338	1	Detroit, Mich.	Capt. Gunnison.	"
5391	1	Brookville, Ind.	Dr. R. Haymond.	"
5348	1	Southern Illinois.	R. Kennicott.	"
5346	2	St. Louis, Mo.	Dr. Engelmann.	"
5531	1	Upper Missouri.	Dr. Hayden.	"
5362	1	Sonora.	Arthur Schott.	"
5435	1	"	J. H. Clark.	Dry.
5432	1	?	?	"
5503	1	?	?	"
5441	1	Sonora.	J. H. Clark.	"

Vespertilio affinis, ALLEN, n. s.

Fig. 48.

Fig. 49.

Description.—Head moderate, slightly depressed; face hairy; ears rather small, inner border convex, outer border concave. Tragus is subulate, about half as high as the ear, straight on internal side, diverging on the external. Lip whiskered. Body robust. Feet long and slender—a few curved hairs at the base of the nails; wing membranes attached midway to base of toes. Interfemoral membrane rather small; a little lobe at the termination of the calcaneum; point of tail exserted. Thumb rather large. Wing membranes dark brown, but thin.

Fur thicker behind than before, and extending a slight distance on the interfemoral membrane. Color lustrous light chestnut-brown above; same color of a lighter shade, inclining to yellowish, below. The base of the fur above and below is of a delicate fawn brown.

The *dentition* is the same as in *V. evotis*—the incisors being of the same length, the laterals bicuspid.

V. affinis resembles *S. georgianus* in being about the same size, and in the fur and membranes presenting the same general appearance. It differs from that species in having the ear more emarginated on the outer border; the tragus not blunt, nor so wide proportionately; the face more hairy, and not so depressed; the reddish hue of the hair more decided; the fur thicker and less wavy. The dentition differs in there being $\frac{6}{6}$ molars, instead of $\frac{5}{5}$. *V. affinis* has also a narrower interfemoral membrane, and a marked calcaneal lobe.

To *V. yumanensis* it bears some resemblance in the shape and extent of the interfemoral membrane, and shape of tragus; but the differences in the pelage, and the color and texture of the wing membranes separate them.

Fig. 50.

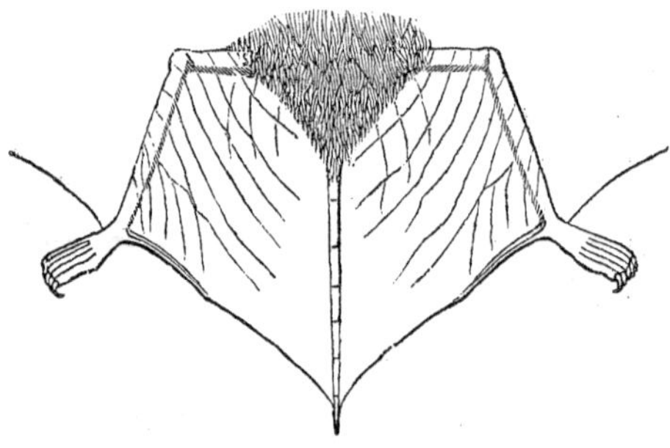

V. affinis.

MEASUREMENTS.

Current number.	Original number.	From tip of nose to tail.	Length of tail.	Length of forearm.	Length of tibia.	Length of longest finger.	Length of thumb.	Height of ear.	Height of tragus.	Expanse.	Nature of specimen.
5342	..	1.1	1.1	1.4	0.6½	2.3	0.4	0.6	0.3	9.0	Alcoholic.

LIST OF SPECIMENS.

Cat. No.	No. of Sp.	Locality.	Presented by	Nature of Spec'm.
5342	1	Ft. Smith, Ark.	Dr. Shumard.	Alcoholic.

No specimens have reached us from any other locality.

Vespertilio lucifugus, LECONTE.

The Blunt-nosed Bat.

Fig. 51.

Fig. 52.

Vespertilio lucifugus, LECONTE, Cuv. An. Kingdom (McMurtrie ed.) I, App. 1831, 431.—IB. Proc. Acad. Nat. Sci. 1855, 436.

Vespertilio brevirostris, MAX PRINCE WIED, Verzeich. beobach. Säug. N. A. 1860, 19.

Description.—Head rather large, somewhat flattish; lips moderately whiskered; snout more obtuse than in other species of *Vespertilio;* nostrils sub-lateral, some distance from free border of upper lip; ears narrow, blunt at tip, slightly emarginated on outer side: the internal basal lobe produced, rounded and somewhat obtuse, not thicker than other portions of ear. Tragus half as high as auricle, mostly blunt, unfrequently abruptly acuminate. Mental space well defined. Feet large; interfemoral membrane of moderate size; termination of calcaneum with interfemoral somewhat abrupt; the point of tail exserted.

Coloration subject to little variation, that of the back dark plumbeous at base, with dark or lightish olive-brown tips; that of the belly lighter at tip—exhibiting a whitish gray, or yellowish gray appearance. The color is thus similar to that of *V. subulatus.*

Dentition as in *V. evotis.*

The narrow blunt ear, short face, and the elevation of the nostril above the free margin of upper lip are the characters which serve to distinguish this species.

V. daubentonii, of Europe, bears some resemblance to this species in the shape of the ear and tragus; but it is dissimilar in the whitish color of fur beneath, and in the attachment of the wing membrane to foot, which is here joined to the ankle instead of the base of the toes as in *V. lucifugus.*

The specimen, numbered 5538, from the east of Colville, N. W. Territory, has a pointed tragus, and the middle part of the free border of the interfemoral membrane fringed with stiff hairs. The fur of the body is silvery beneath, blackish above, back of feet not hairy. Another form from St. Louis, Mo. (Cat. No. 5344), has the wing membrane attached to the ankles—the foot being entirely free. In other respects both agree with *V. lucifugus.*

I have thought it necessary to thus briefly indicate these two aberrant individuals, without giving any separate account of them. Should future collections bring forward any others having the same peculiarities as the above, they may possibly then be thought worthy to receive specific names.

Hab.—Quite common, and universally distributed throughout the United States, and south to the Isthmus of Panama.

MEASUREMENTS.

Current number.	Original number.	From tip of nose to tail.	Length of tail.	Length of forearm.	Length of tibia.	Length of longest finger.	Length of thumb.	Height of ear.	Height of tragus.	Expanse.	Nature of specimen.
5336	..	1.10	1.5	1.5	0 7	2 6	0.2½	0.6	0.2	9.0	Alcoholic.
	..	1.9	1.5		0 6½	2.4	0.2½	0.6	0.3	8.6	"
5353	..	1.9	1.6	1.4	0.4	2.5	0.3	0.7	0.3	8.0	"
5347	..	1.9	1.6	1.4	0 4½	2.5	0 3	0 6½	0.3	8.9	"
5376	..	1.9	1.6	1.4	0 4	2 5	0 3	0.7	0.3	8.9	"
5401	..	2.0	1 6	1.7	0.8	2 6	0.3	0.7	0.4	10 0	"
5364	..	1.6	1.3	1.3	0.6	2 3	0 3	0.6	0 ½	8 0	"
5377	..	1.9	1.3	1.3	0.7	2 2	0.2½	0.6	0.3	9.0	"

List of Specimens.

Cat. No.	No. of Sp.	Locality.	Presented by	Nature of Spec'm.
5376	1	James Bay, Hudson's B.	C. Drexler.	Alcoholic.
5335	1	Westport, N. Y.	S. F. Baird.	"
5334	2	" " ?	" " ?	"
5336	3	Foxburg, Pa.	" "	"
5338	1	Washington, D. C.	" "	"
5337	2	" "	C. Gerard.	"
7197	1	Beaufort, S. C.	Dr. Hayden.	"
7198	1	"	" "	"
5319	1	Isle Royale, Lake Sup.	B. A. Hoopes.	"
5354	1	Detroit River.	S. F. Baird.	"
5501	1	Grosse Isle, Mich.	Rev. C. Fox.	Dry.
5500	1	" "	" "	"
5505	1	" "	" "	"
5373	1	Wisconsin.	A. C. Barry.	Alcoholic.
5498	1	Racine, Wis.	Dr. P. R. Hoy.	Dry.
5349	5	Cook Co., Ill.	R. Kennicott.	Alcoholic.
5497	1	" "	" "	Dry.
5347	2	Cairo, Ill.	" "	Alcoholic.
5363	1	Fort Pierre, Neb.	Dr. Hayden.	"
5379	1	Santa Fé, N. M. [N. N.	W. J. Howard.	"
5374	2	Cantonment Burgwyn,	Dr. Anderson.	"
5361	5	Puget Sound, W. T.	A. Campbell.	"
5366	3	" ? "	Dr. Suckley.	"
5378	2	Fort Steilacoom, W. T.	" "	"
5299	1	Columbia River.	U. S. Exp. Exped.	"
5403	2	Fort Reading, Cal.	Dr. J. F. Hammond.	"
5364	2	" " "	" "	"
5383	2	Cape Flattery, W. T.	Lt. Trowbridge.	"
5380	1	?	?	"
5377	1	?	?	"
5373	1	Aspinwall, N. G.	Dr. S. Hayes.	"

Fig. 53.

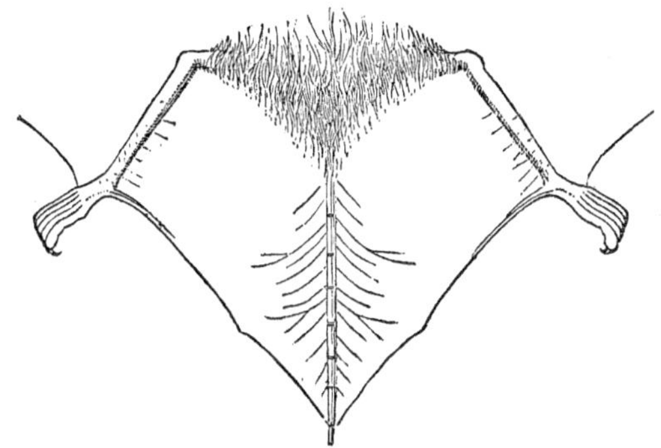

V. lucifugus.

Vespertilio yumanensis, Allen.

The Gila Bat.

Fig. 54.

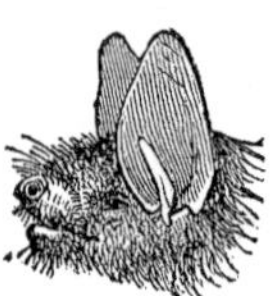

Fig. 55.

Description.—Head moderate, not depressed; hairy. Ears ellipsoid, very slightly emarginated on the outer border. Tragus subulate, half the height of the ear, straight on internal, convex on external border. Nostrils elliptical, opening sublaterally; space between them naked, and slightly emarginated. Lips moderately well covered with whitish whiskers. Body slender. The feet are large, the wing membrane attached midway to the base of the toes. Interfemoral membrane triangular, the termination of the calcaneum forming a lobe with the membrane; the point of tail exserted. The thumb moderate. Wing membranes thin, light color, and almost diaphanous.

The hair behind is plumbeous at base, and light brown at the tip. That in front dark umber at base, and grayish-white at tip—the white hue being predominant. The distribution of fur is the same as in other species.

Dentition same as in *V. evotis.*

In general appearance this bat resembles both *V. subulatus* and *Scotophilus georgianus.* It is, however, smaller than the former, the membranes more delicate, the foot proportionately larger, the interfemoral membrane smaller; but it agrees with it in the subulate tragus, and in the dentition. Its relation to *S. georgianus* is seen in the light brownish snout and ear; its variance therefrom in the longer and more acuminate tragus, the smaller size of the thumb, and the difference in the number of molars.

Hab. This species has not been received from any other locality than the one above given. It was sent to the Institution, from Fort Yuma, with the original type of *Macrotus californicus,* by Major (now Major-General) George H. Thomas, U. S. A.

MEASUREMENTS.

Current number.	Original number.	From tip of nose to tail.	Length of tail.	Length of forearm.	Length of tibia.	Length of longest finger.	Length of thumb.	Height of ear.	Height of tragus.	Expanse.	Nature of specimen.
5367	..	1.6	1.4	1.4	5.0	2.3	0.4	0.6	3.0	9 0	Alcoholic.
6019	..	1.6	1.4	1.3	5.0	2.2	0.4	0.5½	3.0	8.10	"
6020	..	1.6	1.4	1.2	6.0	2.1	0.4	0.5½	3.0	8.6	"
6021	..	1.6	1.4	1.0	6.0	2.2	0.4	0.6	3.0	8.6	"

LIST OF SPECIMENS.

Cat. No.	No. of Sp.	Locality.	Presented by	Nature of Specimen.
5367	36	Ft. Yuma, Cal.	Maj. G. H. Thomas.	Alcoholic.
6019	1	" "	" " "	"
6020	1	" "	" " "	"
6021	1	" "	" " "	"

Fig. 56.

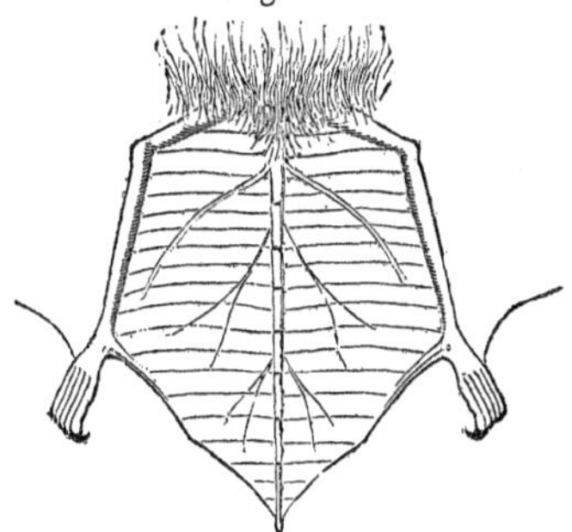

V. yumanensis.

Vespertilio nitidus, Allen.

The Californian Bat.

Fig. 57.

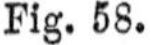

Fig. 58.

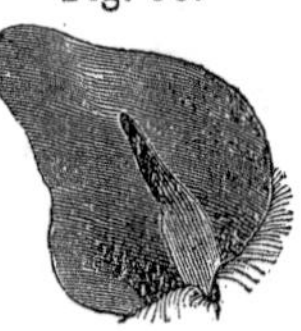

Vespertilio nitidus, Allen, Proc. Phil. Acad. Nat. Sci. 1862, 247.

Description.—Body small; head and face very hairy, the nostrils separated by a narrow, slightly emarginate space; ears longer than head, slightly emarginate on outer edge, curving somewhat outwards, hairy at basal third behind, extending up a greater distance on the inner side; tragus tapering, leaning a little outwards, and about half the height of auricle; lips extensively whiskered; thumb and foot small; interfemoral membrane ample, sparingly haired at upper half behind; calcaneum rather long, with an excalcaneal membrane; color of membranes darkish brown; tip of tail rarely exserted. The termination of the calcaneum forms no angle with the interfemoral membrane.

Fur long and silky. Color plumbeous at base with russet brown and olive tips behind, and lighter russet or ashy cinereous in front. Interfemoral membrane naked, except the usual tuft at the base behind, and a few lightish hairs arranged transversely in front.

Dentition as in *V. evotis*.

This species bears a strong resemblance to *Vespertilio mystacinus*, Leisler, of Europe. The emarginate ear, elongate tragus, and whiskered lips are seen in both; but our species is the larger, while the thumb is smaller; the tail is shorter, and calcaneum more produced. It differs also in color—*V. mystacinus* being of a grayish brown, *V. nitidus* a reddish brown.

Nos. 5405, 5537 and 5402—four specimens in all—present the following peculiarities: The fur is longer than in others of the collection. On the back the base of the hair is blackish; upper third pale yellow, turning to a delicate light-yellowish russet brown; on the belly the hair is dark at the base, with light tips; the hairs on the interfemoral membrane are also of a light color. In other respects the characters are the same as the other specimens. The dried specimen, No. 5512, labelled by Dr. Leconte *V. oregonensis*, though never described by him, probably belongs to this variety. If the individuals having the above coloration should be found to constitute a new species, this name will be reserved for it.

Hab. The species appears, as far as known, to be confined to the regions west of the Rocky Mountains.

Fig. 59.

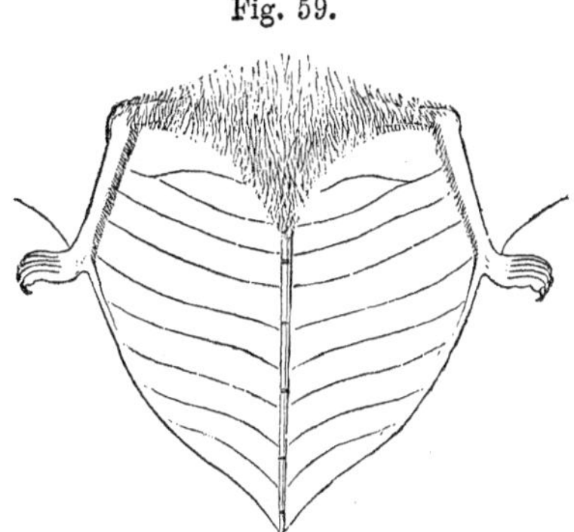

V. nitidus. (Slightly enlarged.)

MEASUREMENTS.

Current number.	Original number.	From tip of nose to tail.	Length of tail.	Length of forearm.	Length of tibia.	Length of longest finger.	Length of thumb.	Height of ear.	Height of tragus.	Expanse.	Nature of specimen.
5433	..	1.8	1.3	1.3	0.6	2.3	0.3	0.5	0.2½	8.0	Dry.
5432	..	1.8	1.0	1.3	0.6	2.0	0.3	0.6	0.3	8 0	"
5446	..	1.6	1.0	1.2	0 6	1.9	0.2	0.4	0.2	7.0	"
523	..	1.7	1.0	1.3	0.6	2.0	0.3	0.5	0.2½	7.9	"
5444	..	1.3	1 1	1.2	0.5	1.9	0 2½	0.4½	0.2½	7.0	"
525	..	1.7	1.2	1.3	0.6	2.0	0.3	0.4½	0.2½	7.7	"
1207	..	1.7	1.2	1.3	0.6	2.9	0.3	0.4½	0.3	?	Alcoholic.
5498	..	1.6	1.5	1.2	0.6	2.0	0.3	0.6	0.3	7.9	"
5500	..	1.7	1.4	1.2	0.7	2.3	0.3	0.5	0.3	8.5	"
5499	..	1.6	1.2	1.2	0.6	2.1	0.3	0.5	0.3	7.9	
5368	..	1.6	1.3	1.2	0.6	2.1	0.1½	0.6	3 0	8 0	"
	..	1.5	1.4	1.1½	0.6	2.1	0 2	0.6	3.0	8.6	"
5535	..	1.6	1.1	1.2	0.6	2.0	0.2	0.6	3.0	7.6	"
5536	..	1.5	1.6	1.2	0.6½	2.1	0.2½	0.6	3 0	8.0	"
5565	..	1.6	1.3	1.3	0.6	2.6	0.2	0.6	3.0	8 0	"
5534	..	1.4	1.2	1.1½	0.5½	2.0	0.1½	0.6	3.0	7.0	"
5537	..	1.5	1.3	1.2	0.6	2.3	0.2	0.6	3.0	8.0	"
5105	..	1.6	1.2	1.2	0.6½	2.1	0.2	0.6	3.0	8.0	"

LIST OF SPECIMENS.

Cat. No.	No. of Sp.	Locality.	Presented by	Nature of Specimen.
5432	1	Guadalupe Cañon, N.M.	Capt. J. Pope.	Dry.
5436	1	Pecos River, Tex.	“ “ “	“
5394	1	Santa Fe, N. M.	W. J. Howard.	Alcoholic.
5536	1	East of Fort Colville.	A. Campbell.	“
5583	6	Puget Sound.	“ “	“
7004	1	“ “	“ “	“
5368	1	Fort Steilacoom, W. T.	Dr. Geo. Suckley.	“
5535	1	“ “ “	“ “ “	“
5444	1	“ “ “	“ “ “	Dry.
5446	1	“ “ “	“ “ “	“
5434	6	“ “ “ ?	“ “ “	Alcoholic.
7005	1	San Francisco, Cal.	R. D. Cutts.	“
5437	1	Monterey, Cal.	W. Hutton.	“
1207	1	“ “	A. S. Taylor.	“
5368	17	Fort Tejon, Cal.	John Xantus.	“
5405	1	Fort Yuma, Ariz.	Maj. Geo. H. Thomas, [U. S. A.	“
5537	2	“ “	“ “	“
5533	1	Cape St. Lucas.	John Xantus.	“
5402	1	“ “	“ “	“
5398	1	“ “	“ “	“

SYNOTUS, KEYSERLING & BLASIUS.

Synotus, KEYSERLING & BLASIUS, Wiegm. Archiv für Naturg. 1839.

Ears very large; outer border extended anteriorly as far as the tragus; large excrescences on either side of the nose continuous with the inner border of the ear; semicircular fold on the base of the outer border of the ear; no tongue-shaped appendage at the base of the inner border, as in *Plecotus*.

The genus *Synotus*, as represented by Keyserling & Blasius, includes both the species found in the United States. It is closely allied to *Plecotus* (a European genus), as both are to *Vespertilio*.

Fig. 60.

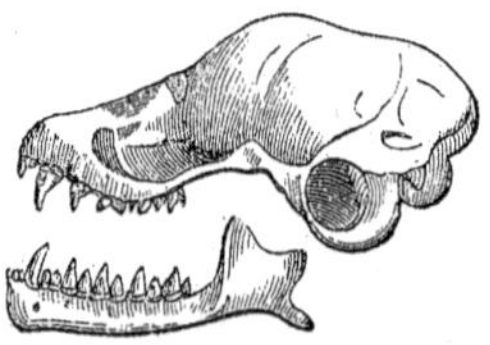

S. macrotis.

Skull.—Rather large. Cranium inflated; a small median depression on the face. No occipital crest.

Dentition.

Molars $\frac{5}{6}$. Canines $\frac{1}{1}$. Incisors $\frac{4}{6}$. Canines $\frac{1}{1}$. Molars $\frac{5}{6}$ = 36 teeth.

Upper Jaw.—Incisors separated by a median space. The centrals larger than laterals, converging, not bifid. The laterals very small and simple. Canines moderate, with a minute basal cusp anteriorly. First premolar very small; second with a large external and small internal cusp. The molars not peculiar.

Lower Jaw.—Incisors minutely trifid. Canines with a minute basal cusp anteriorly. Of the premolars the first and second are small, and about equal; the third much larger though simple.

Synotus macrotis, Allen.

The Big-eared Bat.

Fig. 61. Fig. 62.

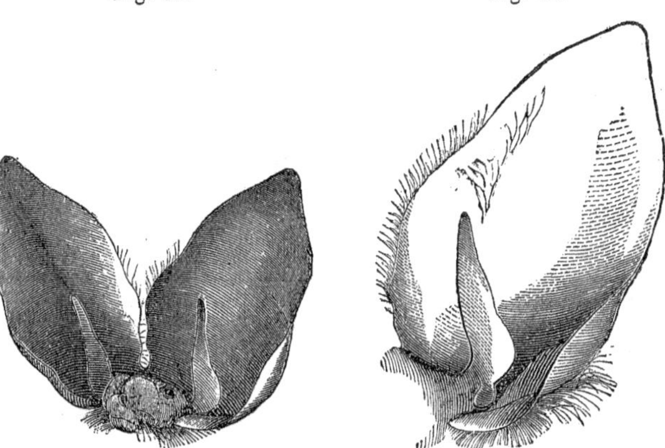

Plecotus macrotis, Leconte, Cuv. Animal Kingdom (McMurtrie ed.), Appendix I, 1831, 431.
Plecotus lecontii, Cooper, Ann. Lyc. N. Y. IV, 1837, 72.
Synotus lecontii, Wagner, Schreb. Säug. V, 1855, 720.

Description.—Head flat, not very broad; face moderately hairy. Lips thin, compressed. Facial crest elevated on a line with the nostrils, which are small apertures with membranous edges, wider externally than internally. They open almost laterally, and have between them a shallow concavity. Ears very large, slightly haired at internal border. The tragus is one-half the height of the ear, straight on the inner edge, diverging on the outer, with a circular lobe at the base almost at right angles to the tragus proper. Hair long, fine and soft. Above it is dark at base—almost blackish; tips dusky, approaching to brown. The base of ear covered with hair—a delicate line extending up the internal border.

The fur of the belly is like that of the back, blackish at base with grayish tips running to white toward the pubis. Interfemoral membrane naked; base of thumb naked. Thumb and foot slender; a few long hairs are seen on the back of the latter.

Originally described by Major Leconte, this species was renamed by Mr. Cooper, as above cited. This naturalist argued that the inappropriate title was sufficient excuse for rendering it obsolete. In reproducing the appellation of Leconte, I consider that, however unfortunate an author's selection of a specific name may be, this alone is no reason why he should be deprived of the right to the priority of the description.

Hab. Confined to the South Atlantic States.

I am informed by Prof. Baird that specimens of a *Synotus*, probably of this species, were received some years ago by the Smithsonian Institution, from Meadville, Pa., but that they have become in some way misplaced and are not now to be found.

MEASUREMENTS.

Current number.	Original number.	From tip of nose to tail.	Length of tail.	Length of forearm.	Length of tibia.	Length of longest finger.	Length of thumb.	Height of ear.	Height of tragus.	Expanse.	Nature of specimen.
5232	..	1.8	1.7	1.7	0.8	2.8	0.4	1.1	0.6	9.6	Alcoholic.
	..	1.8	1.7	?	0.8	2.6	0.4	1.1	0.6	9.4	"
1377	..	1.6	1.6	1.6	0.9	2.8	0.4	1.0	0.6	9.0	Dry.
4727	..	1.9	1.8	1.7	0.9	2.8	0.5	1.2	0.7	11.0	"
890	..	1.10	1.8	1.7	0.8	2.8	0.5	1.1	0.6	10.9	"

LIST OF SPECIMENS.

Cat. No.	No. of Sp.	Locality.	Presented by	Nature of Spec'n.
5451	1	S. Carolina.	W. Cooper.	Dry.
5526	1	S. Carolina.	" "	"
5453	1	Society Hills, S. C.	M. A. Curtis.	"
5450	1	" " "	" "	"
5452	1	Kemper Co., Miss.	D. C. Lloyd.	"
5407	1	Eutaw, Ala.	Prof. Winchell.	Alcoholic.
	1	?	?	Dry.
5234	1	Micanopy, Fla.	Dr. Bean.	Alcoholic.
4727	1	"U. S."	Major Leconte.	Dry.
5232	1	Santa Fe.	W. J. Howard.	Alcoholic.

Synotus townsendi, WAGNER.

Fig. 63.

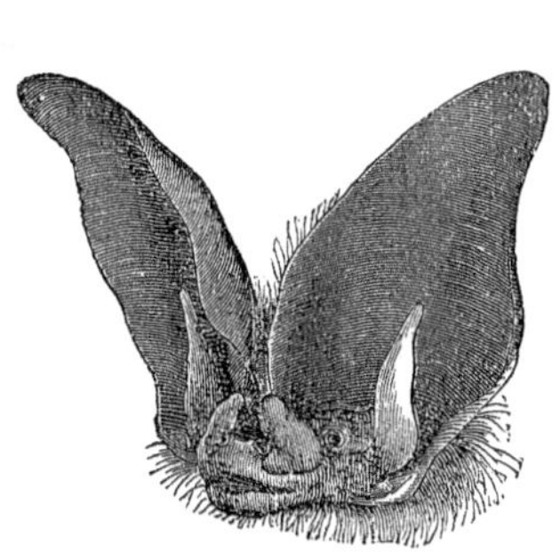

Fig. 64.

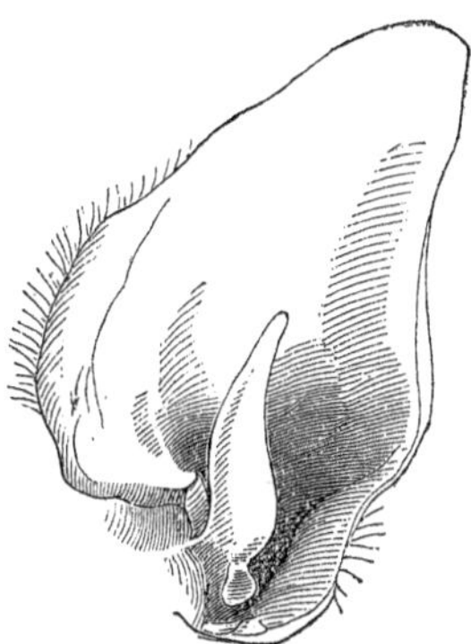

Plecotus townsendi, COOPER, Ann. Lyc. N. Y. IV, 1837, 73.
Synotus townsendi, WAGNER, Schreb. Saüg. V, 1855, 720.

This species resembles the above, but is considerably stouter, the membranes somewhat lighter; face broader and more elongate. The crests are high and well defined, with the wart between the internal border of ear and mouth larger than in *S. macrotis*. The tragus is of the same general shape, with the marked lobe at base. At the lower part of the outer border near the angle of the mouth the small internal lobe is seen as in the preceding species. Limbs slender; thumb and foot rather small.

5

Hair everywhere thick, fine, and long. Brown above, not so markedly bicolored as in *S. macrotis*, but only of a slightly darker hue at base. It is lighter in front, where it assumes a slightly ferruginous brown color at base. The back of the foot but slightly furred. But slight variation in color in the different individuals. Dentition as in the preceding species, excepting that the central incisors of the upper jaw are more distinctly bifid at cutting edge.

Hab. Central region of the United States.

MEASUREMENTS.

Current number.	Original number.	From tip of nose to tail.	Length of tail.	Length of forearm.	Length of tibia.	Length of longest finger.	Length of thumb.	Height of ear.	Height of tragus.	Expanse.	Nature of specimen.
5231	..	1.9	1.9	1.8	0.8	2.10	0.4	1.2	0.7	11.0	Alcoholic.
5230*a*	..	1.9	1.8	1.9	0.8	2.9	0.4	1.3	0.7	11.0	"
5230*b*	..	1.9	1.7	1.9	0.9	2.10	0.4	1.3	0.6	11.0	"
5230*c*	..	1.9	1.9	1.8	0.8	2.9	0.4	1.2	0.6	10.6	"
5230*d*	..	1.9	1.9	1.9	0.8	2.10	0.4	1.2	0.7	10.6	"
5230*e*	..	1.8½	1.9	1.8	0.8	2.11	0.4	1.2	0.6	10.0	"
5230*f*	..	1.9	1.9	1.9	0.9	2.11	0.4	1.3	0.7	11.0	"
5230*g*	..	1.9	1.8	1.8	0.8	2.10	0.4	1.2	0.6	10.6	"

LIST OF SPECIMENS.

Cat. No.	No. of Sp.	Locality.	Presented by	Nature of Spec'm.
5231	1	Upper Missouri.	Dr. F. V. Hayden.	Alcoholic.
5230	7	Utah.	Capt. J. H. Simpson.[1]	"

[1] Collected by C. S. McCarthy.

ANTROZOUS, ALLEN.

Antrozous, ALLEN, Proc. Phila. Acad. Nat. Sci. 1862, 247.

Head rather large; nose high, tapering, narrow; snout angular, blunt; nostrils apical, outer borders joining above in a transverse line; eyes large; ears longer than head, not joined.

Fig. 65.

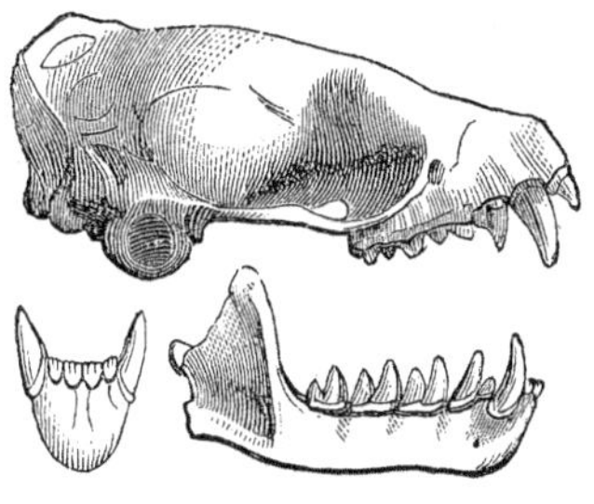

A. pallidus.

Skull long, not depressed, slightly crested at posterior part, tapering anteriorly.

Dentition.

Molars $\frac{4}{5}$. Canines $\frac{1}{1}$. Incisors $\frac{2}{4}$. Canines $\frac{1}{1}$. Molars $\frac{4}{5}$ = 28 teeth.

Upper Jaw.—The superior incisors large, pointed, separated by a narrow space. Canines well developed, with a small basal internal cusp. No small premolar posterior to canine, as in *Lasiurus;* molars as in that genus.

Lower Jaw.—Incisors trilobed, the two centrals placed anteriorly to laterals. Canines with an acute basal cusp which nearly touches the second premolar. The first premolar simple and smaller than the second. Molars not peculiar.

This genus differs from *Vespertilio* in the high and slender snout; the crested and narrow skull; the elevated broad ears, and in having one incisor less on either side in the upper and lower jaw. Indeed, the latter fact is alone sufficient to separate it, for although the incisors in the upper jaw as a general rule are subject to considerable variation, a departure from the usual number in the lower jaw is a matter of more significance. *Antrozous* is the only instance in this extensive family of such variation.

Major Leconte (Proc. Phila. Acad. Nat. Sci. VII, 1855, 437) described a bat from California under the name *Vespertilio pallidus.* The changes which have taken place in the classification of *Cheiroptera* of late years, and especially the greatly restricted sense in which the genus *Vespertilio* is now received, is sufficient apology for the insertion of this bat under the genus above proposed.

Antrozous pallidus, Allen.

The Pale Bat

Fig. 66.

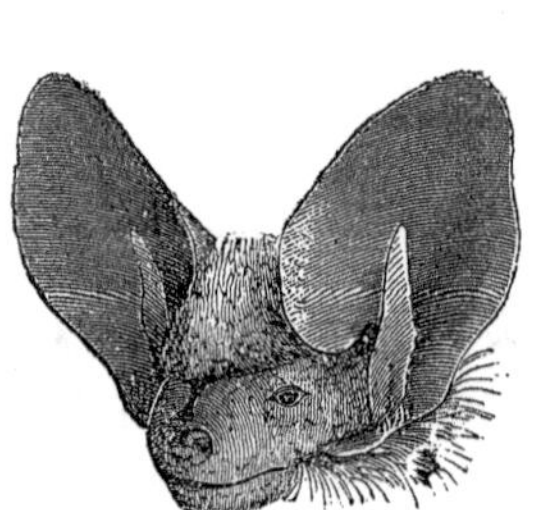

Fig. 67.

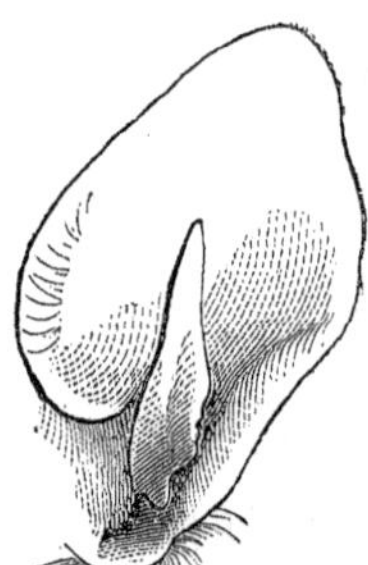

Vespertilio pallidus, Leconte, Proc. Acad. Nat. Sci. VII, 1855, 43.—Baird, U. S. and Mex. Bound. Survey, Report II, 1858, pl. i, fig. 1.

Description.—Head slightly hairy, and of a light brown color. A small wart over each eye; a larger one between outer border of ear and angle of mouth, and another under the lower jaw. Ears high, elliptical, furred at base posteriorly; a slip of fur running up along the inner border; a similar, but narrower slip, running up along the anterior part of the ear. Tragus half as high as auricle, lanceolate, in many instances terminating in a fine point, sometimes in a blunt one; straight on inner border, diverging on outer, where it is finely crenulate. The outer border of the ear does not reach the angle of the mouth by a distance of three lines. Feet rather large; calcaneum moderate.

Two varieties of color are observed in this species—the fawn and the yellowish-brown. The first was the one described by Major Leconte. This author says: "Hair light fawn colored, tip with darker, beneath paler." The yellowish-brown may thus be described: Hair above light brown at base, darker at tips; below lighter brown not tipped. In some instances the brown tip above assumes a reddish tinge, and the fur beneath becomes almost white. The interfemoral membrane is entirely naked. At the base of the thumb a few brown hairs are found.

MEASUREMENTS.

Current number.	Original number.	From tip of nose to tail.	Length of tail.	Length of forearm.	Length of tibia.	Length of longest finger.	Length of thumb.	Height of ear.	Height of tragus.	Expanse.	Nature of specimen.
152	..	2.10	2.0	2.0	0.9	3.0	0.4	0.10	0.6	12.0	Dry.
538	..	2.0	?	2.0	0.8	3.0	0.5	0.9	0.5	10.6	"
521	..	2.4	?	1.10	0.8	3.0	0.5	0.10	0.5	11.0	"
889	..		1.6	2.0	0.9	3.4	0.5	1.0	0.4	11.0	"
887	..	?	?	2.0	0.9	3.0	0.5	0.10	?	?	"
431	..	2.6	?	2.0	0.9	3.4	0.5	0.10	0.6	11 6	"
85	..	2.0	1.6	1.11	1.0	3.0	0.4	0.10	0.6	11.0	"
173	..	2.0	1.6	2.0	1.0	3.0	0.5	0.12	0.7	11.2	"
	..	2.4	1.6	2.0	0.10	3.4	0.5	1.1	0.7	11.6	"
45	..	2.5	1.9	2.0	0.9	3.5	0.5	1.0	0.7	12.0	"

LIST OF SPECIMENS.

Cat. No.	No. of Sp.	Locality.	Presented by	Nature of Spec'n.
152	1	El Paso. (Boundary Sur-	J. H. Clark. (Type.)	Dry.
5241	1	San Elizario, Tex. [vey.)	Dr. C. B. Kennerly.	Alcoholic.
5240	1	Ft. Bliss, N. M.	Dr. S. W. Crawford.	"
5455	1	Ft. Dalles, Oregon.	Dr. Geo. Suckley.	Dry.
538	1	Posa Creek, Cal.	Dr. A. L. Heermann.	"
521	1	Tejon Valley.	" "	"
5238	1	Ft. Tejon, Cal.	John Xantus.	Alcoholic.
5237	5	" " "	" "	"
5239	4	Ft. Yuma, Cal.	Maj. G. H. Thomas.	"
5236	19	Cape St. Lucas.	John Xantus.	"

Fig. 68.

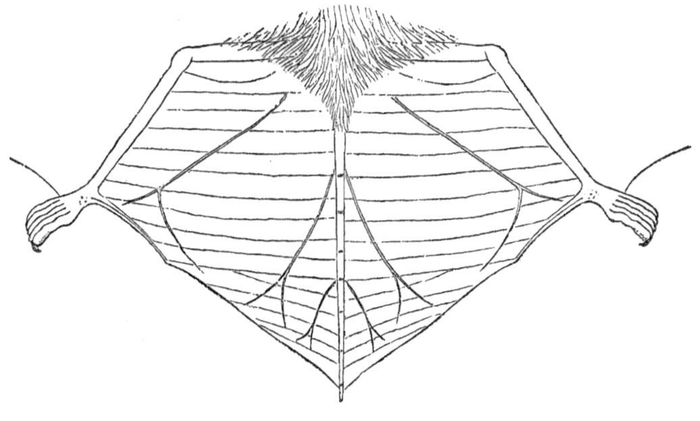

A. pallidus.

APPENDIX.

In order to enable the student to decide for himself in regard to the many doubtful or unidentified species of authors cited in the foregoing pages, the descriptions themselves are reproduced in the present appendix.

A.

Rafinesque.—American Monthly Magazine, III, 1817, 445.

1. *V. mystax.* (Whisker Bat).—Tail two-fifths of total length; upper incisors none, lower 6; two warts at the lower jaw; body entirely fallow, top of the head brownish; ears brown, auriculated, longer than the head. Length, 5 inches; breadth, 14 inches.

2. *V. humeralis.* (Black-shoulder Bat.)—Tail three-sevenths; upper incisors 2, remote; lower 6; body dark brown above, shoulders black; gray beneath; wings, tail, ears, and snout blackish; eyes under the hair; ears longer than the head, elliptical, auriculated. Length, 3½ inches; breadth, 11 inches.

3. *V. tesselatus.* (Netted Bat.)—Tail half of total length, hairy above; upper incisors 2, remote; lower 6; body fallow above, pale dirty fulvous beneath, with a faint fallow collar; shoulders white; wings hairy at the base, with two hairy white spots above near the thumb; membrane blackish, netted of fulvous internally and clotted of same externally; shafts fulvous; nose bilobate; ears nearly concealed by the hair. Length, 4 inches; breadth, 12 inches.

4. *V. cyanopterus.* (Blue-wing Bat.)—Tail one-third; 2 incisors above, 6 below; body dark gray beneath; wings of a dark bluish gray; shafts black; ears auriculated, longer than the head. Length, 3 inches; breadth, 10 inches.

5. *V. melanotis.* (Black-back Bat.)—Tail one-third above, gray beneath; body blackish above, whitish beneath; wings dark gray; shafts black; ears auriculated, rounded. Length, 4¼ inches; breadth, 12½ inches.

6. *V. calcaratus.* (Spurred Bat.)—Tail one-third; body dark brown above, dark fallow beneath; wings black; shafts rose-colored, a spur at the inner side of the elbow; hind feet black. Length, 4 inches; breadth, 12 inches.

7. *V. monachus.* (Monk Bat.)—Tail one-fourth, hairy above, fringed laterally; body pale, fallow above and below; head and neck covered with a longer fur of a dark red fallow; wings dark gray; shafts red; hind feet black; nose red; ears concealed in fur. Length, 4 inches; breadth, 12 inches.

8. *V. phaiops.* (Black-faced Bat.)—Tail one-third of total length, naked, mucronate; body dusky bay above, pale beneath; face, ears, and wings blackish; 4 incisors in the upper jaw—2 on each side, divided by a large flat wart, unequal, the outside ones larger and bilobed; 6 small incisors in the lower jaw. Length, 4½ inches; breadth, 13 inches.

9. *V. megalotis.* (Big-eared Bat.)—Tail three-eighths of total length; body dark gray above, pale gray beneath; ears very large, duplicated, auricles nearly as long. Length, 4 inches; breadth, 12 inches.

B.

RAFINESQUE.—Annals of Nature, 1820, 2.

1. N. sp. *Atalapha fuscata.*—Ears longer than the head, auriculated and blackish; tail three-sevenths of total length, jutting only by an obtuse point; body brownish above, grayish beneath; shoulders and cheeks dark brown; hind feet blackish hairy above; wings blackish brown.—Found in the northern parts of New York, and in Vermont. Total length, 3½ inches. My genus *Atalapha* (Preces des decouvertes Somoliogiques) contain all the bats without fore teeth; there are three or four species of them in the United States all blended under the name of *Vespertilio* (or *Noctilio*) *noveboracensis* by the writers.

I. N. g. *Eptesicus.*—Four acute fore teeth to the upper jaw, in two equal pairs, separated by a great interval and a large flat wart; each pair has two unequal teeth, the outside tooth is much larger and unequally bifid, inside tooth small and entire; six fore teeth to the lower jaw, equal, very small, close and truncate; canine teeth very sharp, curved and long; grinders unequally trifid; snout plain, nose without appendages; ears separated, auriculated; tail mucronate.—This genus appears to differ from all those of Geoffroy and Cuvier, among the extensive tribe of bats. The name means house-flyer.

2. *Eptisecus melanops.*—Fallowish brown above, pale beneath; face, ears, wings, feet and tail blackish; ears oval, shorter than the head, and wrinkled; tail naked, one-third of total length, mucron one-sixth of the tail; posterior toes ciliate.—Not uncommon in Kentucky, Indiana, &c.

Total length, 4½ inches. I had noticed it under the head of *V. phaiops*, in the American Magazine, vol. III. It comes often in the house at night.

3. *Eptisecus mydas.*—Fulvous above, gray beneath; wings, ears, and tail pale brown; shafts whitish; ears double the length of head; tail naked, slightly mucronate, nearly as long as the body.—I have observed it in the barrens of Kentucky, flying in the houses. Total length three inches, of the tail includes five-twelfths. Ears three-quarters of an inch long. I mentioned it under the name of *V. midas*, in my account of the Bats of the Western States (Ann. Mag. vol. III). I have since substituted two other genera of them, *Hypexodon* and *Nycticejus* (Prod. 70, N. G. An.); the others are probably *Atalaphes.* I know already fifteen species of bats in the United States—almost all new ones.

C.

Major Leconte.—Cuv. An. Kingdom (McMurtrie's ed.), 431.

I.

Vespertilio carolinensis, Geof.—Anterior upper fore teeth sub-simple, larger than the posterior. Remarkable for a strong odor resembling that of a fox.

V. lucifugus, L.C.—Anterior upper fore teeth bilobate; body above dark brown, beneath cinereous; nose sub-bilobate; face with a nakedish prominence on each side; ears oblong, naked; tragus sublinear, half as long as the ears; tail projecting a little beyond the membrane. Length, to the insertion of the tail, 2¼ inches; tail 1¼ inches.

V. noctivagans, L.C.—Anterior upper fore teeth bilobate, the posterior sub-simple; color black or dusty cinereous; hair on the back and belly tipped with gray; ears short, naked, roundish; tragus short and roundish; nose sub-bilobate; tail projecting a little beyond the interfemoral membrane, which is hairy. Length, 2⅝ inches; tail, 1⅜ inches.

II.

Add *Plecotus macrotis*, L.C.—Upper fore teeth four, trilobate, distant by pairs, the posterior smaller; ears very long, pointing forwards; tragus subulate, half the length of ears.

III.

Nycticejus noveboracensis.—Easily known by its short and round ears, and by the interfemoral membrane being hairy and including the whole of the tail. There is a white spot at the insertion of the wing, and another at the base of the thumb; these marks are constant. This species varies much in color, and has been called *V. lasiurus*, Schreb., *V. monachus* by some, and is figured in Wils. Orn. VI, pl. 4, whence it has been quoted by M. Cuvier as the *Taphozous.*

Nyc. crepuscularis, L.C.—Above brown, beneath paler; a small black wart above each eye; nose somewhat bilobate; chin with a small double wart; ears moderate; tragus small, subulate; tail projecting a little beyond the membrane.

Nyc. cynocephala, L.C.—The posterior fore tooth on each side smaller than the rest, which are emarginate; nose furnished on the top and sides with stiff short bristles; lips very large, somewhat pendulous; ears broad, round, naked; tragus not apparent; tail long, extending far beyond the membrane; outer and inner toes of the hind feet woolly on the outside, the rest with each two long hairs on the top.

D.

Palisot de Beauvois.—Descriptions of *L. cinereus* and *S. fuscus*, from Pamphlet.

"*Grey Bat.*—Two upper teeth very small, hardly visible. Head whitish; ears round and flat, of a white color surrounded with black, and an appendage at their base; hair grey at the roots, black in the middle, and white at the ends; so that the animal has the appearance of being spotted with white. This hair extends to the membrane which surrounds the tail.

"The anterior parts of the membranous wings from the body of the projecting claw, and covered with hair on both sides. This membrane is about twice the size of that in the preceding species"—(*L. noveboracensis*, Auct.)—"The wings, extended, measure fourteen inches. The nostrils are emarginated.

"Grey Bat. *V. cinereus.*

"This is found in Pennsylvania, and is not described by any author."

"*Brown Bat.*—The two fore teeth in the upper jaw distant from one another, near the canine teeth, and about half their length; ears naked, blackish, and of an oval figure, with an appendage at their base. Tail almost as long as body; flying membrane black; hair brown on the surface, grey below.

"Brown Bat. *V. fuscus.*

"This is the most common species in the neighborhood of Philadelphia. It very much resembles the Common Bat of France, except in the number of teeth in the upper jaw."

E.

Temminck.—Monographie de Mammalogie, II, 1835, 235.

V. ursinus. (A new species kindly furnished me by Prince Max; it is based upon the examination of seven individuals.)—Head large; muzzle rather long, large, and but little depressed; nostrils large, opening upon the side and crescentic—separated by a groove. Ears ovoid, much higher than the summit of the head, the posterior border vertical, and slightly emarginated at the tip; tragus long, lanceolate, but a little rounded near the tip; the auricle is hairy at the base of the external part; the thumb stout, armed by a very curved nail; tail long, point free; interfemoral membrane marked beneath with parallel lines; claws of feet very long, stout, and curved. Incisor teeth above in two close pairs; below 6, trilobed. Molars above 4, without false; inferior with 5, one being a small false molar.

Fur long, soft and shining; above of a brown umber hue, the inferior parts more clear. All the fur is gray at the base. Membranes and ear black.

Length, 3 in. 11 lines—the tail taking 1½ inches; length of ear, 4½ lines; expanse of wing membrane, 10 in. 9 lines.

Hab. Found by Prince Max upon the banks of Missouri River.

V. carolinensis.—Not so large as *V. serotinus* of Europe. Ears as long as the head, oblong, and hairy one-half the length of the external part of ears. Nose a little blunt, but nostrils approached; tragus leaf-shaped, erect, and half as long as the auricle; point of the tail free. Incisors 4, in pairs above, and 6 below. Molars 5 throughout.

Fur bicolored throughout; superior part of a brown "marron," but the base of the hair is ashy black; beneath of a yellow ash, the base of the hair being brown.

Total length, 2, 3 or 5 inches, of which the tail constitutes 1 inch; expanse, 10 inches.

Hab. Charleston, S. C.

V. phaiops.—The general contour like that of *V. murinus.* Point of tail free; tail not so long, strongly "sloped" out on external border, with a lobe cut out behind. Tragus an erect leaf. Superior incisors 4; the external are bilobed, and are larger than the internal. Inferior 6. Molars 4 above and 5 below.

Hair short and unicolored throughout, glossy, above brown, with a tinge of red, below it is of clearer hue; face and membranes blackish.

Length, 4 in. 4 lines, or 5 inches—the tail being 2 inches; expanse of wing membrane, 12 to 13 inches; antibrachium, 1 in. 8 lines.

This is the Black-faced Bat of Rafinesque, of which there is mention made in Desm. Mam. in a note.

Hab. N. A.; our animal comes from Tennessee.

V. pulverulentus.—Resembles, in the color of the superior fur, *V. discolor;* but differs from it in its lesser size, in the interfemoral being hairy on both sides, and in the difference of color of the belly. Muzzle large and obtuse; ears larger than high, rounded, one-half haired; tragus hatchet-shaped; tail short; interfemoral very hairy above, but less at the point than at the base, that beneath of a clear "voie," and in concentric lines; the toes furred above.

Fur long, soft, bicolored throughout, the superior and inferior parts are of the same color. It is of a deep marron, the point only being touched with white, the hairs "clair sermes," arranged in horizontal lines upon the inferior part of the interfemoral membrane, are white.

Length, 3 in. 6 lines, of which the tail is 1 in. 3 lines; expanse, 10 inches; antibrach., 1 in. 6 lines.

This species was furnished us by Prince Max Wied, who obtained it in the mountain recesses of North America. Ours come from the borders of Missouri.

V. caroli.—Tail the form of our *V. pipistrellus*, but the ears are longer. Face obtuse; nostrils very much separated; ears are of medium size, ovoid, slightly emarginate on their external border without having a lobe or prolongation. Upper incisors 4, in pairs above, and 6 below. Molars 6 in all; the two first false molars of the upper jaw very small, short and pointed. Fur bicolored throughout. Face, sides of neck, and all of the superior part of a reddish brown, with black at the base; beneath of a yellowish-white at the point, with a deep brown at base, which in some parts is of a faint yellowish-ash. The young have a more sombre hue. The extreme tip only of the superior parts is brown; that of the inferior is of a deep brown.

Total length, 3 in. 3 lines, the tail of which is 1 in. and 4 lines; expanse of wing membrane, 8 in. 6 lines; antibrachium, 1 in. 4 lines; height of ear from skull to the tip, 5 lines. The young have an expanse of 7 in. 10 lines to 8 inches.

The Museum has obtained from Prince de Musignano—Chas. Bonaparte—many individuals of this species.

Hab. N. America, around the environs of New York and Philadelphia.

V. erythrodactylus.—Less than the *V. pipistrellus.* The forearm, base of fingers, and the interdigital membrane of the first finger is reddish, the other membranes are black. Ears haired from their base the greater portion of their height, small, ovoidal. Tragus subulate; tail very long, point free; interfemoral membrane haired above; beneath the hairs are arranged along the veins; it is of a silky texture, very short, and sparingly distributed. Incisors 4, in pairs above, and 6 below. Five molars in all, only one false molar in the upper jaw.

Fur long, fine and silky; above tricolored, beneath bicolored. All the superior parts of a faint brownish red; but a little yellow about the head and neck; the hairs are black at their base, afterwards yellow and the tip brownish red; superior part of interfemoral membrane very furry; beneath brown at base and brownish red at tip; the sides of the interfemoral covered with sparse hairs.

Length of tail, 2 in. 10 lines, or 3 in. maximum, that of tail 1 in. 4 lines; forearm, 1 in. 2 lines; expanse of wing membrane, 7 in. 6 lines, or 8 in. maximum.

The Museum du Pays Bas possesses many individuals of this supposed new species, for which we are indebted to Prince de Musignano; these specimens are preserved in alcohol, and are part of the same invoice as the preceding species. *Vesp. calcaratus*, indicated by M. Rafinesque, has the wing membranes about the fingers red above; but it is much larger, and the coloration of the fur is considerably different.

Hab. North America, about the environs of Philadelphia.

V. ferrugineus.—Style of *V. daubentonii*, of Europe. Nose short, obtuse; ears narrow, a little scooped out on the posterior border and towards the tip; tragus short, subulate. Tail very long, point free, the basal portion covered with hair; the claws of the hind feet are of a whitish yellow. Upper incisors 4, in pairs, internal long "biseam" at point; the external short, bifurcated; inferior incisors 6. Upper molars 4; lower 5, with one false molar.

Hair short, smooth, bicolored; above the color of a dead leaf, or more or less reddish; the base of the hair is of a brownish black beneath; all the hair at its base is of a faint blackish red, and the point pure white. These two hues of the hair form a sort of black and white mixture which is very conspicuous. The membranes of the ears, having been immersed in alcohol, are of a brownish red.

Total length, 4 in., or 2 lines longer, that of the tail 1 in. 9 lines; humerus, 1 in.; forearm, 1 in. 8 lines; anal expanse, 10 in. or 6 lines longer.

This species, based upon the examination of many alcoholic specimens, is new.

Hab. Holland Guiana. (Museum *Pays Bas:* from the environs of Surinam.)

F.

Say.—Long's Expedition to the Rocky Mts. II, 65, note.

Vespertilio subulatus.—A small bat was shot this evening, during the twilight, as it flew rapidly in various directions over the surface of the creek. It appears to be an immature specimen, as the molars are remarkably long and acute; the canines are very much incurved, and the right inferior one is singularly bifid at tip—the divisions resembling short bristles. This species is, beyond a doubt, distinct from the Carolina Bat (*V. carolinensis*, Geof.), with which the ears are proportionately equally elongated, and, as in that bat, a little ventricose on the anterior edge, so as almost to extend over the eye; but the tragus is much longer, narrower, and more acute, resembling that of *V. emarginatus*, Geof., as well in form as in proportion to the length of the ear. We call it *V. subulatus*, and it may be thus described: Ears longer than broad, nearly as long as the head, hairy on the basal half, a little ventricose on the anterior edge and extending near to the eye; tragus elongated, subulate; the hair above blackish at base, tip dull cinereous; the interfemoral membrane hairy at base, the hairs unicolored, and a few also scattered over its surface, and along its edge, as well as that of the brachial membrane; hair beneath black, the tip yellowish-white; hind feet rather long, a few setæ extending over the nails; only a minute portion of the tail protrudes beyond the membrane.

Total length, 2 9-10 inches; tail, 1 1-5 inches.

G.

M. F. Cuvier.[1]—Nouv. Annales du Museum d'Hist. Nat. 1832, 15.

1. *Vespertilio gryphus.*—The head is like that of the *Murinoid* group of bats. To the molars proper of which is united two additional false molars on both sides of either jaw. The ear is emarginated, and the tragus is knife-shaped. All the superior parts of the body are of a whitish yellow, the inferior parts are gray, but the base of the fur on both sides is of a blackish color. Whiskers are present on each side of the upper lip and on the extremity of the lower jaw.

Length of body, from the tip of nose to base of tail, 1 in. 9 lines; length of tail, 1 in. 2 lines; expanse of wing membranes, 7 in. 10 lines.

Hab. Environs of New York. (M. Milbert.)

2. *V. salarii.*—The head is like that of the *Murinoid* group of bats. To the molars proper of which is united the presence of two false molars on both sides of either jaw. The ear is emarginate, and the tragus lanceolate. The superior parts of the body are of a brown chestnut-gray, and the inferior parts a grayish white. There is more of the brown color at the basal portion of the fur than at the upper. Whiskers are present on the sides of the upper lip and at the extremity of the lower jaw.

Length of body, from tip of nose to the base of tail, 1 in. 6 lines; length of tail, 1 in. 7 lines; expanse of wing membranes, 7 in. 7 lines.

Hab. Environs of New York. (M. Milbert.)

3. *V. creeks.*—The head of the *Serotinoid* group of bats. No false molars on upper jaw, and one only inferiorly; the ear is emarginate, the tragus lanceolate; the upper parts are of a brown yellow, the inferior parts of a dirty gray; the hairs of all the parts are black at their base. Whiskers are present on the sides of the muzzle and beneath upon the lower jaw.

Length of body, from tip of nose to the base of the tail, 2 inches; length of tail, 1 inch; expanse of wing membranes, 9 inches.

Hab. Georgia. (Major Leconte.)

---

[1] M. Cuvier designated by the term "*Murinoid group*" those species of Cheiroptera since placed under the genus *Vespertilio*. In the "*Serotinoid group*" he placed those species now included in *Scotophilus*. The names are taken respectively from two well known European species—*V. murinus* and *V. serotinus*.

4. *V. crassus.*—The head is like that of the *Murinoid* group of bats. Two false molars on each side of the two jaws; the ears are obtuse, the tragus is lanceolate. All the superior parts of the body of a brown chestnut-gray, and the inferior parts whitish; the fur at its base is darker tinted than its tips. Moustaches are present on the upper lip and upon the lower jaw.

Length of body, from tip of nose to base of tail, 2 inches; length of tail, 1 in. 8 lines; expanse of wing membranes, 8 in. 8 lines.

This species was collected by M. Leseuer, who sent it from New York, under the name which I have retained.

5. *V. georgianus.*—The head is like that of the *Murinoid* group of bats. The ear is emarginate, and the tragus is subulate. All the superior parts of the body are colored by a mixture of black and whitish yellow; the black mostly, inasmuch as the points of the hair are whitish, the remainder being black. The inferior parts are gray, but mixed with black from the same cause which colors the superior portions. Moustaches are present on the sides of the upper lips and upon the lower jaw.

Length of body, from tip of nose to base of tail, 1 in. 6 lines· length of tail, 1 in. 2 lines; expanse of wing membranes, 7 in. 2 lines.

Hab. Georgia. (Major Leconte.)

6. *V. subflavus.*—The head is like that of the *Murinoid* group of bats. The ear is emarginated, the tragus is half heart-shaped. The inferior parts of the body are of a clear whitish-gray, slightly waved with brown; the superior parts are of a white yellow; the hairs of the superior parts are black at their base, whitish through the greater part of their length, and brownish at their tips; that of the inferior parts are black at their basal portions, and of a whitish yellow at their outer. Moustaches are present on the sides of the upper lip and beneath upon the lower jaw.

Length of body, from tip of nose to the base of the tail, 1 in. 6 lines; length of the tail, 1 in. 3 lines; expanse of wing membranes, 7 in. 2 lines.

Hab. Georgia. (Major Leconte.)

H.

J. J. AUDUBON and the Rev. JOHN BACHMAN, D. D.—Journal Acad. Nat. Sci. Phila. 1842, 280.

Vespertilio monticola. (Mountain Bat.)—V. vespertilione subulata brevior; auriculus brevioribus; tragus non excedentibus, dimidian longitudinem auriculæ; colore fulvo.

Mountain Bat.—Smaller than Say's Bat—("*V. subulatus*")—ears shorter; tragus less than half the length of the ear; color yellowish-brown. Upper fore teeth bilobate; ears moderate, naked, erect, rather broad at base; tragus linear, subulate; body small; wings long; tail projecting a line beyond the interfemoral membrane, which is slightly sprinkled with hair above and beneath.

Color.—The nose and chin are black; ears light brown; wing membranes dark brown. The whole of the fur of the body above and beneath is, from the roots, a uniform delicate brown color.

This species differs from Say's Bat, not only in color but in the much shorter ears and tragus. The size and shape of the tragus we have found an invaluable guide in our American bats; the ears of the present species, when alive, are always erect; whilst those of Say's Bat are folded backwards like those of the long-eared bats—*Plecotus.*

Dentition.—Incisors $\frac{2-2}{6}$. Canines $\frac{1-1}{1-1}$.

Dimensions.—Length of head and body, 1 in. 8 lines; length of tail, 1 in. 6 lines; height of ear, 3 lines; height of tragus, $1\frac{1}{4}$ lines.

N. B.—The tragus in Say's Bat is four and a half lines in height. Several specimens of this bat were obtained during the summer, on the mountains of Virginia at the Gray Sulphur Springs. They were uniform in size and color.

V. virginianus. (Virginian Bat.)—V. vespertilione monticola paululum longior, auriculus paululum longioribus magisque acutis; dentibus primoribus maxillæ superioris simplicibus; interfemorali membrana nuda; corpore supra fuligineo-fusco; subtus cinereo-fuscato.

Virginian Bat.—A little larger than the Mountain Bat; ears a little longer and more pointed; upper fore teeth simple; interfemoral membrane naked; sooty brown above, ash brown beneath.

Dentition.—Incisors $\frac{2-2}{6}$. Canines $\frac{1-1}{1-1}$.

In size this species is intermediate between *V. carolinensis* and *V. subulatus.* The ear is naked, less rounded, and more pointed than either of the other closely allied species. The tragus is very narrow, linear, and less than half the length of the ear. The tail is inclosed in the interfemoral membrane, except the penultimate joint, which is free. The anterior upper fore teeth, instead of being sub-simple, as in the *V. carolinensis*, or bilobate, as in *V. subulatus* and *V. montanus*, are simple.

Color.—The nose, upper lip, and upper jaw are black; wings dark brown. The back is sooty brown; on each shoulder, at the insertion of the wing, there is a circular black spot about four lines in diameter; on the under surface cinereous brown.

Dimensions.—Length of head and body, 2 in. 5 lines; length of tail, 1 inch; height of ear, 4 lines; height of tragus, $1\frac{3}{4}$ lines.

Hab. Mountains of Virginia.

V. leibii. (Leib's Bat.)—V. supra fusco-ferrugineus, subtus cinereus, alis auribusque nigris.

Leib's Bat.—Ears and wings black; dark yellowish-brown above; cinereous beneath.

Description.—Anterior upper fore teeth bilobate; head short; nose blunt; ears moderate, broad at base, erect; tragus nearly linear, nearly half the length of the ear; wings and tail long, the latter extending two lines beyond the interfemoral membrane, which is naked; feet very small; toes short and slender; nails sharp and much curved; hair soft and downy.

Color.—The ears, wings, and interfemoral membrane are black. The fur on the back is black from the roots to near the extremities, where it is so slightly tipt with light brown as to give it a dark yellowish-brown appearance. On the under surface the hairs are plumbeous at the roots, tipt with yellowish-white.

Dentition.—Incisors $\frac{2-2}{6}$. Canines $\frac{1-1}{1-1}$.

Dimensions.—Length of head and body, 1 in. 7 lines; length of tail, 1 in. 4 lines; length of spread, 7 inches; height of ear, 2½ lines; height of tragus, 1 line.

Hab. Michigan.

V. californicus. (Californian Bat.)—V. fusco lutescens, vellere longo et molli; trago longitudine dimidium auris excedente.

Californian Bat.—With long silky hairs; tragus more than half the length of the ear; color light yellowish-brown.

Description.—Anterior upper fore teeth bilobate. Head small; nose sharp; ears of moderate size, erect, rather narrow, and pointed. Tragus linear, attenuated. Wings of moderate length, which, together with the ears, are naked. Interfemoral membrane with a few scattered hairs; feet small; nails slightly hooked. Tail projecting a little beyond the interfemoral membrane.

Color.—Pelage, which is unusually long for the size of the body, and very soft and glossy, is, on the upper surface, dark plumbeous from the base, and broadly tipped with light yellowish-brown; on the under surface the color is a little darker, owing to the outer extremities of the hairs being more narrowly edged with the prevailing color on the back, exhibiting the darker shades beneath. The ears and tragus are blackish; the nose, chin, wings, and interfemoral membrane dark brown.

Hab.—We have obtained but a single specimen, which was captured at California.

Dentition.—Incisors $\frac{2-2}{6}$. Canines $\frac{1-1}{1-1}$.

Dimensions.—Length of head and body, 1 in. 7 lines; length of tail, 1 in. 5 lines; length of spread, 7 in. 6 lines; height of ear, 3 lines; height of tragus, 2 lines.

I.

Prince Maximil. von Wied.—Verzeich. beobach. Säugethiere in Nord Amerika, 1862, 19.

Vespertilio brevirostris.—Description: Head very short; snout broad, and but little produced; ear tolerably high, rather elliptical, the anterior border somewhat rounded, the outer nearly straight, under the tip slightly emarginated; tragus rather small, nearly lancet-shaped; the fur about the head very plentiful, so that the eyes are entirely hidden.

Dentition.—The specimen of this bat is lost, so I cannot therefore furnish the dentition.

The expansion of the wings rather small. Thumbs long and small, with greatly curved nails. Tail somewhat long, eight or nine joints lying on the outer half of the fur of the interfemoral membrane, the tip, however, is one and a half to two lines long, with the free points exserted; the five hind toes are long, the nails weak, and sharply curved; calcaneum rather long; fur thick about the belly, mouse-like, that of the back longer; wing membranes near the body are somewhat furred.

Coloration.—Expansion of wing membranes and ears are dark brown; upper portion of the body dark yellowish-brown, the hair on the outer half fallow yellowish-brown, dark gray at the roots; under portion whitish yellow-gray.

Measurements.—Entire length, 3 inches; expanse of wing membrane, 9 in. 4 lines; height of ears on the upper side 5½ lines; length of the exposed portion of the tragus, 1½ lines; the tail is free from the fur about 1 in. 5 lines; length of calcaneum, 5 lines.

I obtained this bat at Freiburg, Pennsylvania, about the latter part of July. It flies about rather early in the morning. We have observed that this bat resembles the other species closely, but it is readily distinguished by the shortness of the head, as the name given to it implies.

INDEX.

www.ingramcontent.com/pod-product-compliance
Lightning Source LLC
LaVergne TN
LVHW021427110826
845150LV00007B/2121

* 9 7 8 1 4 2 5 5 0 7 6 7 1 *